RAND Environment, Energy, and Economic Development Program

T0302514

Links Between Air Quality and Economic Growth

Implications for Pittsburgh

Shanthi Nataraj, Ramya Chari, Amy Richardson, Henry H. Willis

Prepared for the Heinz Endowments

The research described in this report was sponsored by the Heinz Endowments and conducted in the Environment, Energy, and Economic Development Program within RAND Justice, Infrastructure, and Environment.

Library of Congress Cataloging-in-Publication Data

Nataraj, Shanthi.
Links between air quality and economic growth : implications for Pittsburgh / Shanthi Nataraj, Ramya Chari, Amy Richardson, Henry H. Willis.
pages cm
Includes bibliographical references.
ISBN 978-0-8330-8399-9 (pbk. : alk. paper)
1. Air pollution—Economic aspects—Pennsylvania—Pittsburgh. 2. Air quality—Economic aspects—Pennsylvania—Pittsburgh. I. Title.

HC108.P7N38 2013
363.739'20974886—dc 3

2013049208

The RAND Corporation is a nonprofit institution that helps improve policy and decisionmaking through research and analysis. RAND's publications do not necessarily reflect the opinions of its research clients and sponsors.

Cover image: Pittsburgh skyline (Andy Truello, via WikiMedia Commons; CC BY 2.0).

RAND OFFICES

SANTA MONICA, CA • WASHINGTON, DC

PITTSBURGH, PA • NEW ORLEANS, LA • JACKSON, MS • BOSTON, MA

DOHA, QA • CAMBRIDGE, UK • BRUSSELS, BE

www.rand.org

Preface

This report presents the results of a RAND Corporation study for the Heinz Endowments. The study sought to better characterize the links between air quality and economic development to help understand how improving air quality in the Pittsburgh region could affect local economic growth. The findings presented here are based on a review of the existing, national studies on links between air quality and economic growth and on an extrapolation of some of those results to the Pittsburgh region; the findings were also informed by discussions with individuals engaged in economic development and air pollution policy from the private, public, and nonprofit sectors. The findings should be of interest to local policymakers, individuals, and organizations working in the areas of economic development and environmental policy.

The RAND Environment, Energy, and Economic Development Program

The research reported here was conducted in the RAND Environment, Energy, and Economic Development Program, which addresses topics relating to environmental quality and regulation, water and energy resources and systems, climate, natural hazards and disasters, and economic development, both domestically and internationally. Program research is supported by government agencies, foundations, and the private sector.

This program is part of RAND Justice, Infrastructure, and Environment, a division of the RAND Corporation dedicated to improving policy and decisionmaking in a wide range of policy domains, including civil and criminal justice, infrastructure protection and homeland security, transportation and energy policy, and environmental and natural resource policy.

Questions or comments about this report should be sent to the project leader, Henry Willis (Henry_Willis@rand.org). For more information about the Environment, Energy, and Economic Development Program, see http://www.rand.org/energy or contact the director at eeed@rand.org.

Contents

Figures

Tables

Summary

Although Pittsburgh, Pennsylvania, is still often referred to as the "Steel City," the region has diversified its industrial base toward service-oriented industries, such as education and health care. At the same time, the Pittsburgh region's air quality has improved during the past several decades. But although industrial soot no longer blots out the sun, the region still faces challenges with air pollution. For example, Pittsburgh remains out of compliance with some of the National Ambient Air Quality Standards (NAAQS) for criteria air pollutants set by the U.S. Environmental Protection Agency (EPA). In addition, EPA's national-scale air toxicity assessment indicates that Allegheny County (in the Pittsburgh metropolitan statistical area [MSA]) ranked 63 out of 3,141 U.S. counties in overall cancer risk, 123 in overall neurological risk, and 327 in respiratory risk related to air toxicity (EPA, 2013c).[1]

The primary reason to improve air quality is to achieve better health outcomes, such as reduced instances of bronchitis, asthma, and premature mortality. Improving air quality has its costs, including the capital and operation and maintenance costs to businesses that are required to install pollution control equipment, as well as the costs of regulations related to improved fuel economy. Despite some controversy over the exact nature of the costs and benefits, the total value of benefits from major clean air legislation has been shown to exceed the costs substantially (EPA, 2011a).

It is also possible that improving air quality may affect the economic performance of a local area, by improving the health of the workforce, contributing to overall quality of life, affecting business costs (via the impacts of local air quality on local regulations), or through other channels. This report examines the relationship between air quality and economic growth through three pathways:

- **Pathway 1: Health and related workforce issues and costs.** This effect links air quality to the health of the local population and subsequently to effects on the health and productivity of the local workforce. Workforce productivity and health can affect business costs and productivity, and thus local economic growth.

[1] These rankings include risks based on air toxics, not criteria air pollutants. Note that a lower number indicates a higher risk; a ranking of 1 would indicate the county with the highest risk.

Figure S.1
The Pittsburgh Metropolitan Statistical Area

SOURCES: U.S. Department of the Interior and U.S. Geological Survey, undated; Office of Management and Budget, 2013.
RAND *RR260-S.1*

- **Pathway 2: Quality-of-life issues and location decisions.** Air quality may affect quality of life for residents, either directly or through health effects. In turn, quality of life may influence business and residential location decisions, thus affecting growth.
- **Pathway 3: Air quality regulations and business operations.** The stringency of national air quality regulations varies with local air quality. Local areas with better air quality face less stringent regulations, and that affects cost and location decisions for certain businesses.

How air quality influences local economic growth through each of these pathways and how this information is relevant to the Pittsburgh region are critical but seldom-addressed questions. Discussions of air quality improvements often focus on health outcomes (on the benefit side) and direct costs (on the cost side). By highlighting some of the links between improved air quality and impacts on workforce productivity, individual relocation decisions, and business operations, policymakers, local organizations, and others interested in air quality and local growth in the Pittsburgh region and elsewhere can engage in a new kind of dialogue that more directly links environmental and economic well-being.

Study Methods

The three pathways were identified through a rigorous review of existing economic and environmental literature. The evidence for each pathway was assessed based on the literature review. Pathways 1 and 3 were then examined quantitatively by extrapolating results from existing studies to the Pittsburgh region, to provide a sense of the local economic value associated with achieving the NAAQS. For pathway 1, improvements were estimated using several health-related metrics that would be associated with improving air quality to meet the NAAQS. For pathway 3, the fact that areas that fail to meet the NAAQS face more-stringent air quality regulations, which, in turn, affect business location and operation decisions, was considered. The changes in the number of establishments, employment, and output in selected industries that would be associated with meeting the NAAQS were estimated.

In order to assess pathway 2, as well as specific aspects of pathways 1 and 3, the team conducted semistructured interviews with representatives of 27 organizations in the Pittsburgh region and elsewhere. Interviewees included representatives of 11 firms in pollution-intensive and non–pollution-intensive industries and universities; eight community groups and academics; three government agencies involved in both environment and development issues; and five local and national site selection firms and recruiters.

How Does Air Quality Affect the Health of the Local Population?

For pathway 1, reducing concentrations of particulate matter less than 2.5 microns in diameter ($PM_{2.5}$) from 2012 levels to the current NAAQS would be associated with health improvements valued at approximately \$488 million (Table S.1). Similarly, reducing ozone concentrations from 2012 levels to the NAAQS would be associated with health improvements valued at \$128 million (Table S.2). These values are driven

Table S.1
Annual Effect of Meeting the Particulate Matter Standard on Key Health Endpoints in the Pittsburgh Metropolitan Statistical Area

Endpoint	Incidence Mean (number of avoided cases)	Valuation ($ thousands)
Acute bronchitis	72	27
Acute myocardial infarction	9	446
Asthma exacerbation	1,526	238
Chronic bronchitis	42	6,405
Emergency-room visits, respiratory	38	10
Hospital admissions, cardiovascular	16	414
Hospital admissions, respiratory	18	402
Adult mortality	89	486,185
Upper-respiratory symptoms	1,323	35
Work loss days	7,243	857
Total		487,793

SOURCE: Authors' calculations using EPA's BenMAP software, with ambient air quality values updated to reflect 2012 concentrations in the Pittsburgh MSA.

NOTE: The total valuation is based on a Monte Carlo simulation of the underlying results for each endpoint and is therefore not equal to the sum of the individual valuations. The selection of endpoints relies on EPA's selection of epidemiological studies available in BenMAP.

largely by the values associated with reduced premature adult mortality.[2] Estimates for ozone are based on the current NAAQS of 75 parts per billion (ppb), but it should be noted that, in 2010, EPA proposed lowering the NAAQS to 60 to 70 ppb and subsequently drafted documents for a revised standard of 70 ppb. As of October 2013, however, EPA reported that it was continuing its five-year review of the NAAQS (EPA, 2013i).

Meeting the NAAQS for $PM_{2.5}$ would include improvements in a health-related metric that may be particularly salient to local business: work-loss days. In addition, meeting the NAAQS for ozone would reduce school-loss days, which, in turn, reduces work-loss days. In Table S.2, one school-loss day is valued at the lost wages that a parent faces from taking time off to care for a sick child. The team confirmed that these find-

[2] Our estimates were developed using BenMAP, a geographic information system–based program provided by EPA.

Table S.2
Annual Effect of Meeting the Ozone Standard on Key Health Endpoints in the Pittsburgh Metropolitan Statistical Area

Endpoint	Incidence Mean (number of avoided cases)	Valuation ($ thousands)
Emergency-room visits, respiratory	14	5
Hospital admissions, respiratory	26	832
Mortality	18	128,267
School loss days	5,600	566
Total		127,635

SOURCE: Authors' calculations using EPA's BenMAP software, with ambient air quality values updated to reflect 2012 concentrations in the Pittsburgh MSA.

NOTE: The total valuation is based on a Monte Carlo simulation of the underlying results for each endpoint and is therefore not equal to the sum of the individual valuations. The selection of endpoints relies on EPA's selection of epidemiological studies available in BenMAP.

ings were robust to a range of assumptions about the baseline incidence rates of work- and school-loss days.

How Do Air Quality Regulations Affect Business Operations?

For pathway 3, existing evidence indicates that, if an area is not in attainment with the NAAQS (called *nonattainment*), firms in certain regulated industries may find it more difficult to locate or to grow in that area. The team drew on results from a national study showing that counties that are in attainment with the ozone NAAQS have more establishments in regulated industries. By extrapolating these results to Pittsburgh, the team found that, in the Pittsburgh MSA, being out of attainment with the NAAQS is associated with approximately eight fewer establishments in regulated industries. Meanwhile, being out of attainment with the ozone and $PM_{2.5}$ NAAQS is associated with approximately 1,900 and 400 fewer jobs, respectively, and with $229 million and $57 million less in output from regulated industries, respectively (Table S.3).

The analysis presented here is subject to certain limitations. First, when extrapolating national results to the Pittsburgh region, the team assumed that the relationship between air quality or air quality regulations and the percentage change in a metric that was identified in the literature could be applied to the Pittsburgh region. Those percentage changes were then applied to Pittsburgh-specific baseline data on the metrics. This assumption is consistent with the way in which health benefit estimates are typically constructed (EPA, 2011a). Second, it should be noted that coming into com-

Table S.3
Estimated Effect of Not Being in Attainment on Regulated Industry Outcomes in the Pittsburgh Metropolitan Statistical Area

Pollutant	Estimated Fewer Establishments in Regulated Industries in the Pittsburgh MSA	Estimated Fewer Jobs in Regulated Industries in the Pittsburgh MSA	Estimated Reduction in Output from Regulated Industries in the Pittsburgh MSA ($ millions)
Ozone	8	1,914 to 1,946	229
TSP	Not applicable	413	57

SOURCE: Authors' calculations based on extrapolating estimates from Henderson (1996) and Greenstone (2002) to the Pittsburgh MSA.

NOTE: TSP = total suspended particulates. Pollutants examined for each outcome are based on those considered in the underlying studies.

pliance with the NAAQS entails costs on regulated industries; estimating the costs of coming into compliance was outside the scope of this study.

Summary of Findings

The team did not conduct a cost-benefit analysis and thus cannot make specific policy recommendations. However, the project did elicit three significant findings:

- **Improved local air quality would have substantial health-related benefits for the Pittsburgh region** (pathway 1). Meeting the NAAQS can reduce incidences of various health outcomes, such as premature mortality, emergency-room visits, and work-loss days. This could result in an annual benefit of $128 million for reducing ozone from 2012 levels to the NAAQS or of $488 million for reducing $PM_{2.5}$ from 2012 levels to the NAAQS.
- **Cleaner air may affect workers' location decisions** (pathway 2). There is suggestive evidence that people "vote with their feet" to live in places with cleaner air, particularly when it comes to local relocations. Although there is less empirical evidence on how air quality affects intercity migration decisions, the team's stakeholder interviews offered anecdotal evidence that recruiters use all possible tools when convincing potential employees to move to a particular city. The fact that the Pittsburgh region does not meet national air quality standards thus removes one potential tool from recruiters' toolkits. Encouraging local human resource departments in Pittsburgh-area firms to gather information from applicants about what factors played a role in their decisions to accept or reject an offered job or using recruiting or survey data to examine the reasons that candidates from other

parts of the country would or would not be willing to consider taking a job in the Pittsburgh region could be important next steps in understanding the impacts of the Pittsburgh region's air quality on its potential to attract future residents.

- **Businesses in regulated industries may have an easier time locating and growing in the Pittsburgh region once air quality standards are met** (pathway 3). Although regulated industries do face costs associated with improving air quality, meeting the NAAQS can make it easier for businesses in regulated industries to locate and operate in the Pittsburgh region in the long run. In the Pittsburgh region, being designated as in attainment with the NAAQS ozone standard would be associated with eight more establishments, 1,900 more jobs, and $229 million more output in regulated industries; being in attainment with the NAAQS $PM_{2.5}$ standard would be associated with 400 more jobs and $57 million more in output from regulated industries.

Acknowledgments

We would like to thank the representatives of the companies, community organizations, real estate and site selection firms, recruiting firms, academic institutions, government agencies, and other individuals who shared their experiences and opinions with us. We thank the Heinz Endowments for their insightful comments on earlier drafts, as well as Court Gould at Sustainable Pittsburgh for his input during the interviews. Neal Fann at the U.S. Environmental Protection Agency provided advice and guidance on the BenMAP software we used to conduct an analysis of health outcomes. We are indebted to Shanti Gamper-Rabindran, Jill E. Luoto, Richard D. Morgenstern, Ward Thomas, and Hua Wang for their helpful comments and suggestions on a draft version of this manuscript. We also thank John Graham for his review of issues related to air quality data and analysis. Omar Al-Shahery, Lauren Andrews, and Aviva Litovitz provided excellent research assistance. Any remaining errors are the responsibility of the authors.

Abbreviations

μg	microgram
BACT	Best Available Control Technology
CFC	chlorofluorocarbon
CMU	Carnegie Mellon University
CR	concentration response
DEP	Pennsylvania Department of Environmental Protection
DPM	diesel particulate matter
ECO	Electronic Collections Online
EPA	U.S. Environmental Protection Agency
GDP	gross domestic product
GIS	geographic information system
HAP	hazardous air pollutant
HQ	hazard quotient
LAER	lowest achievable emission rate
LRI	lower-respiratory illness
m^3	cubic meter
MSA	metropolitan statistical area
NAAQS	National Ambient Air Quality Standards
NATA	National-Scale Air Toxics Assessment
NAICS	North American Industrial Classification System

NO_2	nitrogen dioxide
NO_x	nitrogen oxide
OR	odds ratio
PDE	Pennsylvania Department of Education
PM	particulate matter
$PM_{2.5}$	particulate matter less than 2.5 microns in diameter
PM_{10}	particulate matter less than 10 microns in diameter
ppb	part per billion
ppm	part per million
PSA	particle strong acidity
R&D	research and development
SIC	Standard Industrial Classification
SLD	school-loss day
SO_2	sulfur dioxide
SO_4	sulfate
SO_x	sulfur oxide
TFP	total factor productivity
TRI	Toxics Release Inventory
TSP	total suspended particulates
VNA	Voronoi neighbor averaging
VOC	volatile organic compound
WLD	work-loss day
WTP	willingness to pay

CHAPTER ONE

Introduction

Historically, Pittsburgh was a stronghold of the iron and steel industries in the United States and was known first as the Iron City and then as the Steel City. The city's population grew from 322,000 in 1900 to more than 675,000 by 1950, but subsequently declined, as did the local iron and steel industries. Although manufacturing remains an important component of the local economy, Pittsburgh has more recently diversified its industrial base toward more service-oriented industries, such as education and health care. In 2010, the city's population was approximately 306,000, while the Pittsburgh metropolitan statistical area (MSA) had an estimated 2.4 million residents ("Pittsburgh," undated). Mean household income in the MSA was approximately $68,000 in 2012, while per capita income was $29,000 (U.S. Census Bureau, 2012c). The top four industries in terms of employment in 2011 were health care and social assistance (18 percent); retail trade (12 percent); accommodation and food services (9 percent); manufacturing (9 percent); professional, scientific, and technical services (7 percent); and educational services (6 percent) (U.S. Census Bureau, 2012b). In terms of output, the largest industries in 2007 were wholesale trade, manufacturing, retail trade, and health care and social assistance (U.S. Census Bureau, 2012c).

Concurrently with a shift toward a more service-oriented economy, and similar to many other cities in the United States, the Pittsburgh region has also seen improvements in its air quality during the past several decades. However, the Pittsburgh region remains out of compliance with key requirements of the Clean Air Act.

The Clean Air Act was originally passed in 1970 "to protect and enhance the quality of the Nation's air resources so as to promote the public health and welfare and the productive capacity of its population" (42 USC 7401). It was subsequently amended in 1977 and 1990. One of its central provisions requires the U.S. Environmental Protection Agency (EPA) to set National Ambient Air Quality Standards (NAAQS) for common air pollutants, known as *criteria pollutants*. EPA sets both primary standards, aimed at protecting human health, and secondary standards, aimed at environmental issues, such as visibility and damage to crops and buildings. Currently, EPA regulates six criteria pollutants: carbon monoxide, lead, nitrogen dioxide (NO_2), ozone, particle pollution, and sulfur dioxide (SO_2) (EPA, 2012).

In regulating criteria pollutants, EPA designates areas (typically counties) as being *in attainment* or *out of attainment* (also known as *nonattainment*) with the NAAQS for each pollutant. States are required to develop plans, known as *State Implementation Plans*, for improving air quality in nonattainment areas and for preventing degradation in attainment areas. Nonattainment area plans must typically include more-stringent control measures for new or expanding sources.

In addition to the NAAQS, the Clean Air Act addresses hazardous air pollutants (HAPs). EPA regulates 187 HAPs based on the weight of scientific evidence suggesting that exposure to these air pollutants may result in serious adverse health outcomes, including cancer, reproductive and developmental effects, immunological impairments, and neurological and respiratory ailments (EPA, 2013e). Examples of HAPs include benzene, dioxin, asbestos, and metal compounds (e.g., mercury, chromium, cadmium). HAPs may arise from a variety of different sources, including mobile sources (e.g., cars) and stationary sources (e.g., factories), as well as indoor sources and consumer products (e.g., building materials, paint, cleaning solvents).

Other provisions of the Clean Air Act specifically address acid rain, ozone-depleting substances, and haze that impairs visibility in national parks.

Criteria Pollutants in the Pittsburgh Region

Most of the seven-county Pittsburgh MSA is out of attainment with the NAAQS for two criteria pollutants: ozone and particulate matter. In addition, smaller areas within the region are also out of attainment with the NAAQS for sulfur dioxide and lead.

The entire seven-county Pittsburgh MSA is designated as a single nonattainment area (called the Pittsburgh–Beaver Valley area) for ozone (Figure 1.1).[1] The current ozone NAAQS is 75 parts per billion (ppb); this standard is applied to the fourth-highest, daily maximum eight-hour concentration, averaged over three years. EPA reports these three-year averages as *design values* and typically uses design values to determine whether an area is in attainment with the NAAQS. For the Pittsburgh–Beaver Valley area, the design value for ozone from 2010 to 2012 was 82 ppb, above the NAAQS of 75 ppb (EPA, 2013f).

Our estimates for ozone are based on the current NAAQS, but we note that, in 2010, EPA proposed lowering the NAAQS to 60 to 70 ppb and subsequently drafted documents for a revised standard of 70 ppb. As of October 2013, however, EPA reported that it was continuing its five-year review of the NAAQS (EPA, 2013i).

Nearly all of the MSA is also out of attainment with the NAAQS for particulate matter less than 2.5 microns in diameter ($PM_{2.5}$) (Figure 1.2). In the case of $PM_{2.5}$,

1 The seven counties in the Pittsburgh MSA (Allegheny, Armstrong, Beaver, Butler, Fayette, Washington, and Westmoreland) are all designated as out of attainment with the 2008 eight-hour ozone standard.

Figure 1.1
Designated Eight-Hour Ozone Nonattainment Areas in Pennsylvania and Neighboring States, 2008 Standard

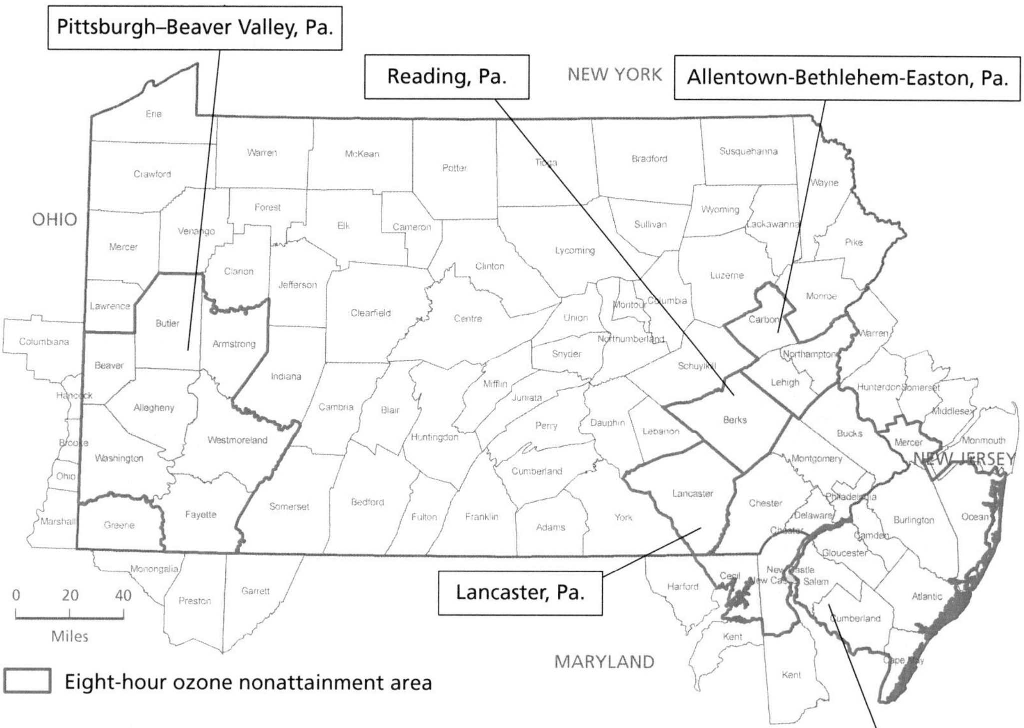

SOURCE: EPA, 2013d.
NOTE: The map shows areas designated by EPA as being out of attainment with the 2008 eight-hour ozone standard. ppm = part per million.
RAND *RR260-1.1*

most of the MSA falls under the Pittsburgh–Beaver Valley nonattainment area; however, the Lincoln, Clairton, Glassport, Liberty, and Port Vue boroughs in Allegheny County make up the Liberty-Clairton nonattainment area, which has typically experienced higher $PM_{2.5}$ concentrations than the surrounding areas.[2] The current nonattainment designations for $PM_{2.5}$ are based on the 2006 annual standard of 15 micrograms per cubic meter (μg/m^3) (applied to the mean, averaged over three years) and a daily standard of 35 μg/m^3 (applied to the 98th percentile, averaged over three years). However, the annual standard was lowered to 12 μg/m^3 in 2012.

[2] The Pittsburgh–Beaver Valley $PM_{2.5}$ nonattainment area includes Allegheny County (except for the boroughs that are in the Liberty-Clairton nonattainment area); Elderton, Plumcreek, and Washington Townships in Armstrong County; Beaver County; Butler County; Washington County; and Westmoreland County. In addition, the area includes two townships outside of the Pittsburgh MSA (Monongahela Township in Greene County and the township of Taylor, south of New Castle City, in Lawrence County).

Figure 1.2
Designated $PM_{2.5}$ Nonattainment Areas in Pennsylvania, 2006 Standard

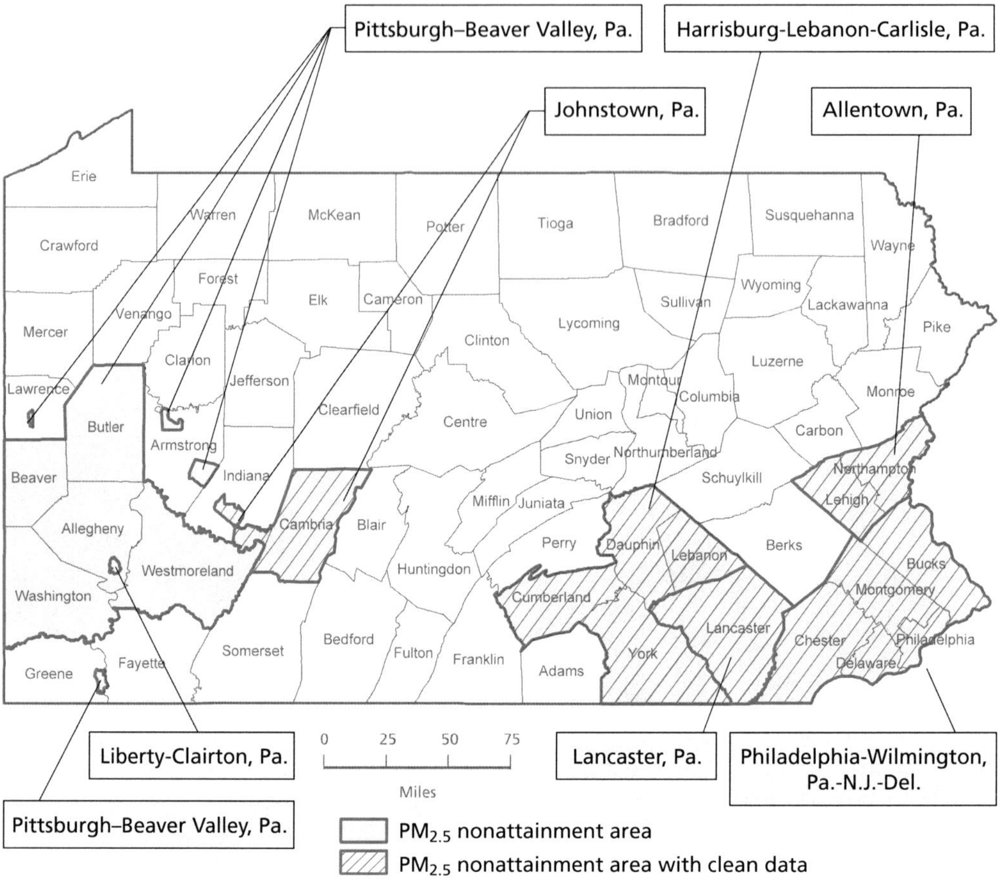

SOURCE: EPA, 2013d.
NOTE: Areas designated by EPA as being out of attainment with the 2006 standard for $PM_{2.5}$.
A "clean data" designation indicates that EPA has determined that the area is in attainment.
RAND *RR260-1.2*

As shown in Table 1.1, for Liberty-Clairton, the 2010–2012 design value for daily $PM_{2.5}$ was 43 μg/m^3, substantially above the daily standard of 35 μg/m^3. The 2010–2012 design value for daily $PM_{2.5}$ in Pittsburgh–Beaver Valley, 33 μg/m^3, was just below the NAAQS. In addition, the 2010–2012 design value for annual $PM_{2.5}$ in the Liberty-Clairton nonattainment area was 14.8 μg/m^3, while the annual design value for the Pittsburgh–Beaver Valley nonattainment area was 12.6 μg/m^3 (EPA, 2013g). Although these annual values are at or below the previous NAAQS of 15 μg/m^3, each is above the current standard of 12 μg/m^3. EPA will not formally make the nonattainment designations until 2014, but the 2010–2012 design values suggest that both regions would have been considered out of attainment based on the last three-year cycle.

Table 1.1
Design Values for 2010–2012 for Two $PM_{2.5}$ Nonattainment Areas in the Pittsburgh Metropolitan Statistical Area, Micrograms per Cubic Meter

$PM_{2.5}$ Measure	NAAQS	Liberty-Clairton	Pittsburgh–Beaver Valley
Daily	35	43	33
Yearly	12	14.8	12.6

SOURCE: EPA, 2013g.

The ozone and $PM_{2.5}$ NAAQS are health-based, meaning that the standards are set using protection of public health as the guiding decision criterion. Exposure to ozone is associated with exacerbation of asthma and respiratory illness, hospital admissions and emergency-department visits for respiratory causes, school absences, and mortality. The majority of ground-level ozone is formed from photochemical reactions between volatile organic compounds (VOCs) and nitrogen oxides (NO_x). VOCs are emitted from multiple sources, including chemical plants, gasoline pumps, and paints. Major sources of NO_x include power plants and motor vehicles (EPA, 2013a). $PM_{2.5}$ is associated with numerous health effects, including acute and chronic bronchitis, asthma exacerbations, hospital admissions, and upper respiratory symptoms. In addition, evidence indicates that $PM_{2.5}$ is associated with cardiovascular disease, mortality from cardiovascular and respiratory causes, and work-loss days (WLDs). $PM_{2.5}$, or fine particulate matter (PM), is a mixture of particles and liquid droplets found in air that are less than 2.5 microns in diameter. The small size of fine PM is a concern because of the particles' ability to penetrate deeply into the lungs. Major $PM_{2.5}$ sources include fuel combustion from motor vehicles, diesel-powered vehicles, power plants, and industrial processes (EPA, 2009).

Hazardous Air Pollutants in the Pittsburgh Region

The Pittsburgh region also experiences high concentrations of toxic air pollutants, or HAPs. In a 2009 report, Carnegie Mellon University (CMU) researchers detailed the results of an analysis of adverse health effects expected in the Pittsburgh region due to pollutant exposures for 65 air toxics (CMU, 2009). The authors performed risk assessments comparing four monitoring sites and estimated both lifetime cancer risks and noncancer hazard quotients (HQs) (the ratio of potential exposure to a substance and the level at which no adverse effects are expected to occur) for individual and grouped toxics: organics, metals, polycyclic organic matter, and diesel particulate matter (DPM). Of these four classes, DPM showed the greatest cancer risks overall (across all four sites), and the highest risks were found in the downtown Pittsburgh monitoring site. Additive cancer risks for all pollutant classes exceeded the one-in-1-million threshold (one cancer case per 1 million population) that EPA typically uses as guidance for determining acceptable population risk. Additive risk for DPM in the downtown Pittsburgh site was estimated to be as high as one in 1,000. Noncancer health risks were determined through calculation of HQs: HQs greater than 1 indicate that adverse health effects are possible. Only one air toxic, acrolein, was estimated to pose a chronic noncancer risk to health.

EPA uses the National-Scale Air Toxics Assessment (NATA) to identify and prioritize air toxics, emission sources, and locations that may be of concern. In the 2005 NATA (EPA, 2013c), Allegheny County ranked 63rd out of 3,141 U.S. counties in overall air toxics–related cancer risk, 123rd in overall neurological risk, and 327th in respiratory risk. These rankings include risks based on air toxics, not criteria air pollutants. Note that a lower number indicates a higher risk; a ranking of 1 would indicate the county with the highest risk.

Aims of This Report

The primary reason to improve air quality is to achieve better health outcomes, such as reducing instances of bronchitis, asthma, and premature mortality. Other benefits include improved plant growth, reduced damage to structures, reduced acidification of freshwater bodies, and improved visibility. Improving air quality also has its costs; those costs include the direct capital and operation and maintenance costs to businesses that are required to install pollution control equipment; the costs of meeting the motor vehicle tailpipe and fuel rules and conducting vehicle inspections; and indirect costs, such as productivity losses. Despite some controversy over the exact nature of the costs and benefits, the total value of benefits from major clean air legislation has been shown to exceed the costs substantially (EPA, 2011a).

It is also possible that improving air quality may affect the economic performance of a local area, by improving the health of the workforce, contributing to overall quality of life, affecting business costs (via the effect of local air quality on local regulations), or through other channels.

Ideally, we would like to identify the *causal* impact of improving local air quality on local economic growth (measured, for example, in terms of gross regional product). However, rigorously identifying this effect is challenging because of the complex links between air quality and economic growth. On one hand, local economic growth may affect air quality. For example, growth may be driven by an increase in heavy manufacturing output with a related increase in emissions or by a shift away from heavy manufacturing toward service industries, which could reduce emissions.[3] On the other hand, local air quality could affect economic growth if cleaner air attracts workers to a region.

Our aim was to identify the pathways from air quality to economic growth. Therefore, given the challenges discussed above, we reviewed the existing literature and identified three pathways through which local air quality could influence local economic growth: health and workforce issues, health and quality-of-life issues, and air quality regulations and business activities. This report addresses these questions: What evidence exists for how air quality influences local economic growth through each of these pathways? How might those effects be relevant to the Pittsburgh region?

We extrapolated some of the existing results to the Pittsburgh region, to provide a sense of the economic value associated with achieving the NAAQS. For the health and workforce pathway, we estimated improvements in several health-related metrics that would be associated with improving air quality to meet the NAAQS.[4] For the business activity pathway, we considered the fact that areas that fail to meet the NAAQS face more-stringent air quality regulations; these regulations have been shown to affect business location and operation decisions. We therefore estimated changes in the number of establishments, employment, and output in selected industries as metrics for the value of meeting the NAAQS. These benefits must be balanced against the cost of meeting the NAAQS, which we do not address in this report.

The remainder of this report is organized as follows. In Chapter Two, we describe the methodology we used in conducting this research, including key limitations. Chapter Three outlines three key channels through which air quality could influence economic growth through its influence on firm and individual decisions, and it summarizes our assessment of the existing literature for each of those channels. In Chapter Four, we present the results of our extrapolation of existing results to the Pittsburgh region, and Chapter Five concludes. In addition, we provide five appendixes: a summary of the literature reviewed, our interview protocol, a review of site selection processes, detailed health benefit estimates, and industry codes referenced in the report.

---

3 Another potential way in which growth could affect air quality is if people demand cleaner air as their incomes rise (in other words, if clean air is a normal good). See, for example, Carson, Jeon, and McCubbin (1997) and List and McHone (2000), who study the relationship between per capita income and pollution across states.

4 Our estimates were developed using BenMAP, a geographic information system (GIS)–based program provided by EPA.

CHAPTER TWO

Methodology

We searched the existing literature to identify and assess the evidence for potential links between air quality and economic growth. We also conducted interviews with stakeholders in the Pittsburgh region and elsewhere. These interviews complemented our literature search in two ways. First, we used the interviews to identify whether there were other critical links we had not yet identified through our literature search. Second, we used our interviews to gauge which specific links might be most applicable to the Pittsburgh region.[1] We then extrapolated evidence from selected studies to the Pittsburgh region, using baseline outcome data from the local area.

In this chapter, we describe each of these methods, including the associated limitations.

Literature Review and Synthesis

We conducted targeted searches of relevant academic databases and journals to identify evidence on existing links between air quality and economic growth. These databases included Business Source Premier, EconLit, Electronic Collections Online (ECO), Medline, and Social Sciences Abstracts.

We worked with a RAND research librarian to identify appropriate search strings for each database. We do not provide an exhaustive list of search terms, but we present a sample of the types of search strings used:

- (air quality OR air pollution OR clean air) AND (business OR economic growth OR economy OR employment OR labor OR jobs OR workforce OR location decision)
- (air quality OR air pollution OR clean air) AND (worker productivity OR work loss days OR child absent OR school absenteeism OR school loss days)

---

1 For example, there is a substantial literature on effects of air quality on agriculture and forest productivity (EPA, 2011a). However, given our interviews, we decided not to focus on this link; it is not particularly relevant to the Pittsburgh MSA.

- (air quality OR air pollution OR clean air) AND (tourism OR recreation)
- (air quality OR air pollution OR clean air) AND (housing prices OR willingness to pay OR hedonic).

We tried a variety of permutations using alternative terms for air pollution (e.g., "ozone" and "particle pollution"), as well as for outcomes of interest (e.g., "cost of illness" or "employer health cost"). We modified the search strings as necessary to meet the requirements of each database.

The titles of potentially relevant articles were entered into a database. Team members screened the list of titles and selected potentially relevant articles, for which we obtained abstracts. We then obtained the full text of articles deemed relevant based on a review of their abstracts.

We complemented our search of academic databases in two ways. First, once we had identified relevant articles from academic databases, we conducted a "snowballing" process, in which we identified additional articles based on the reference lists of relevant studies. During our interviews (discussed below), a few stakeholders also recommended potential articles for inclusion.

Second, we conducted a search of several nonacademic or "grey literature" sources. These sources included databases of unpublished academic literature (e.g., working-paper series from the National Bureau of Economic Research), as well as reports by government agencies (e.g., EPA, Congressional Research Service) and policy organizations (e.g., Resources for the Future). We identified material through a search of key organization websites, as well as a general Google Scholar search using search terms similar to those listed above.

A full systematic review of the literature was beyond the scope of this study. Nonetheless, once we had identified potentially relevant articles, team members reviewed them based on the "weight of evidence" framework of Gough (2007). The framework judges the study in three areas:

- weight of evidence A: Is the study well-executed? We considered such factors as whether the study assumptions are likely to be met, whether there is an assessment of the quality of the data, whether there is a discussion of the possible biases and their directions, and whether sensitivity analyses are performed.
- weight of evidence B: Is the method used in the study relevant to the link being examined?
- weight of evidence C: Is the topic focus or context of the study relevant to the link being examined?

For those articles identified as appropriate for inclusion, we captured key elements of the study in question. Appendix A lists the studies that we included in our assessment of existing evidence, including a summary of the pollutant or regulation studied, the key outcomes, the main methods and assumptions, and the key findings. We then developed a narrative synthesis to summarize our findings from the literature.

Limitations

A key limitation of our literature review is that we may have missed relevant articles, despite our search of various databases. In addition, because we did not conduct a full systematic review or a quantitative analysis (such as a meta-regression analysis) of the evidence for each link, our synthesis of the evidence should be interpreted as providing guidance about which links might be important for further study, rather than as rigorous evidence about the magnitude or statistical significance of results associated with the links.

Stakeholder Interviews

We conducted semistructured interviews with representatives of 27 organizations in the Pittsburgh region and elsewhere. Interviewees included representatives of 11 firms in pollution-intensive and non–pollution-intensive industries and universities; eight community groups and academics; three government agencies involved in both environment and development issues; and five local and national site selection firms and recruiters. Within each organization, we spoke with different people, including human resource representatives, managers, and environmental specialists. We often spoke with more than one person within each organization, and the specific questions we asked were tailored to the interviewee's role.

The interviews, which typically lasted about an hour, began with a brief introduction of the study. At the start of each interview, we informed the respondent that his or her comments were not for attribution to individuals or to the organization he or she represented. In most cases, two to three members of the research team conducted the interviews, with one person primarily responsible for taking notes.

The interview protocol is provided in Appendix B. This protocol served as a guide for semistructured interviews; rather than following a specific order of questioning, we adapted the questions and discussion to the specific interviewee and his or her responses. The protocol covered the following areas:

- general perceptions about air quality and economic development
- the extent to which air quality or air quality regulations affect firm location decisions
- the extent to which air quality or air quality regulations affect firms' day-to-day operations and employment
- the extent to which air quality or air quality regulations affect worker recruiting or retention, or specific choice of residence

- the extent to which air quality or air quality regulations affect tourism and broader regional issues, including ecosystems and agriculture
- links between air quality and regional planning issues, such as transportation.

Limitations

The key limitation of this method is that, even though we aimed to conduct interviews with a broad range of stakeholders, the interviewees are not meant to be representative of the local Pittsburgh or national population. Interviewee responses may have been shaped by personal experience and attitudes about air quality and economic development. As such, we did not use the results of our stakeholder interviews in assessing the evidence for links between air quality and economic growth. Rather, we used the interviews to ensure that we had not missed any potentially important links between air quality and economic growth in our literature search and to identify links that might be particularly salient for future study in the Pittsburgh region.

Extrapolation of Health Benefit Estimates to the Pittsburgh Region

We used EPA's BenMAP 4.0 software to estimate how meeting the NAAQS for ozone and $PM_{2.5}$ would affect key health outcomes and to value those outcomes. BenMAP is a GIS-based software tool that contains information about air pollution levels, air pollution–related health effects, and local populations in the United States and that allows users to estimate the health outcomes and values associated with changing air quality.

We began by examining the value associated with several major health endpoints, including reduced premature mortality, respiratory illnesses, and cardiovascular disease. We then conducted a more detailed analysis of the value associated with two health endpoints that may have an immediate outcome on local business: WLDs and school-loss days (SLDs).

We used health impact functions to estimate the expected changes in health outcomes associated with attaining the standards for $PM_{2.5}$ and ozone. Health impact functions relate changes in outcomes to changes in ambient air concentrations of pollutants. They typically consist of four components: a concentration-response (CR) function determined from epidemiological studies, a baseline incidence rate for the outcomes of concern, the estimated change in air pollutant concentrations, and the affected population numbers. The results from the health impact function are then combined with valuation data to determine the value of the improved health outcomes. Each of these steps is described in more detail below.

Concentration-Response Functions

The CR function is the relationship between the pollutant and the outcome. For example, one common assumption in many epidemiological studies is that the relationship between adverse outcome and $PM_{2.5}$ or ozone pollution is best described as log-linear, in which the natural logarithm of the outcome response is a linear function of pollutant concentration (Abt Associates, 2012). In this case, the change in number of outcomes (*O*) of endpoint *J* when ambient concentrations (*C*) of $PM_{2.5}$ or ozone change can be given by

$$\Delta O^J = \left[\exp\left(\beta^J \times \Delta C\right) - 1\right] \times O_0^J \times Pop^J, \tag{1}$$

where β^J is the CR coefficient of endpoint (e.g., SLD or WLD) and O_0^J is the baseline incidence rate of endpoint *J* in the affected population, Pop^J. Because β^J is small, Equation 1 can be linearized and expressed as the following:

$$\Delta O^J = \beta^J \times O_0^J \times \Delta C \times Pop^J. \tag{2}$$

Linear and logistic are other forms that are commonly assumed to describe the pollutant-outcome relationship.

In our analysis, we relied on EPA's selection of epidemiological studies for the choice of the CR functions to use in the benefit analysis (Abt Associates, 2012). EPA's selected studies assessed the relationship between $PM_{2.5}$ and acute bronchitis, acute myocardial infarction, asthma exacerbation, chronic bronchitis, emergency-room visits for respiratory illness, hospital admissions for cardiovascular and respiratory illnesses, mortality, and upper-respiratory symptoms and WLDs; they also assessed the relationship between ozone and emergency-room visits for respiratory illness, hospital admissions for respiratory illnesses, mortality, and SLDs. In general, EPA's selection of studies included considerations of the study design and location, characteristics of study populations, and whether studies were peer-reviewed. Whenever more than one primary study was identified, we pooled the study-specific estimates of incidence change by random-effects inverse weighting. The random-effects pooling method takes into account both within-study and between-study variance in incidence estimation; studies with lower standard errors are given greater weight in the final pooled estimate.

Baseline Incidence Rates

Baseline incidence rates for health outcomes are needed to translate the relative risk of the effect, derived from the CR function, to the absolute change in effect, or the number of avoided cases per year. For our baseline analysis, we used default incidence rates from BenMAP. For our more detailed analysis of WLDs, we used three separate incidence rates from BenMAP: the incidence in large MSAs, the Midwest, and the

Northeast. These data were obtained from the Centers for Disease Control and Prevention's 2010 National Health Interview Survey (Centers for Disease Control and Prevention, 2012) and represent ages 18 to 64.

For the more detailed analysis of SLDs, we identified incidence rates from two sources. First, we drew on the Pennsylvania Department of Education (PDE) child accounting data files (2008–2009), which include estimates of annual child absences for all Pennsylvania counties (PDE, 2009). We aggregated county data to determine SLD incidence for the Pittsburgh MSA. These data are relevant to the whole MSA but include SLDs for all causes, so they are likely to overestimate SLDs due to respiratory illnesses. We also gathered data from the Pittsburgh public schools on SLDs due to medical leave and sickness. Although these data are specific to the city of Pittsburgh and therefore may not be representative of the MSA, they are likely to be closer to the SLD rate due to respiratory illness.

Air Pollution Exposure

Selecting Monitor Data and Spatial Interpolation

BenMAP 4.0 includes monitor values for $PM_{2.5}$ and ozone from 2000 to 2007. We uploaded 2012 data for the analysis from EPA's Air Quality System (EPA, 2013h). Because monitor data reflect conditions only in very localized areas (i.e., in the areas near the monitor), we used Voronoi neighbor averaging (VNA) to interpolate monitor data across unmonitored areas of the Pittsburgh MSA. The VNA algorithm calculates an inverse-distance weighted average of values from monitors that closely surround predefined grid areas of a certain size.

Reducing $PM_{2.5}$ and Ozone Levels to Standard Levels

To determine the benefits associated with a reduction in $PM_{2.5}$ and ozone levels, we first needed to specify how air quality might improve in the Pittsburgh MSA to achieve the NAAQS. The NAAQS for $PM_{2.5}$ and ozone consist of a standard level, averaging time, and form:

- yearly $PM_{2.5}$: annual mean standard of 12 µg/m^3, averaged over three years
- daily $PM_{2.5}$: 98th-percentile 24-hour value of 35 µg/m^3, averaged over three years
- ozone: annual fourth-highest daily maximum eight-hour concentration of 75 ppb, averaged over three years. EPA recently proposed a lower standard (70 ppb); we used the current NAAQS because the proposed standard is not final.

To meet the NAAQS, we assumed that the annual mean $PM_{2.5}$ concentration could not exceed 12 µg/m^3, that the 24-hour mean $PM_{2.5}$ concentration could not exceed 35 µg/m^3, and that the fourth-highest, eight-hour maximum ozone concentration could not exceed 75 ppb. We represented attainment metrics in a simplified form by using the most recent year of data available instead of averaging across three years. We used a maximum form for the daily $PM_{2.5}$ standard instead of the 98th percentile.

BenMAP offers a range of methods for reducing (referred to as *rolling back*) out-of-attainment monitors, including percentage (or proportional), incremental, quadratic, and peak-shaving. Informed by our discussions with EPA representatives, we decided to focus our analysis on the percentage-reduction approach because anticipated control strategies in the Pittsburgh MSA for the next five to ten years (e.g., programs targeting regional emissions and ozone-precursor emissions) appear to be best modeled by this approach.[2]

We then defined baseline and control scenarios in the Pittsburgh MSA for $PM_{2.5}$ and ozone. The baseline scenario reflected conditions before any reductions were initiated, while the control scenario was determined using the selected monitor reduction methods. We set monitor values to the specified standards while accounting for background pollutant concentrations (pollutant concentrations not attributable to anthropogenic sources). Background pollutant concentrations are assumed to be unaffected by any air pollution control strategy and are therefore not adjusted using reduction methods. We assumed a constant background of 3 $\mu g/m^3$ for $PM_{2.5}$ yearly and daily standard metrics and backgrounds of 0, 40, and 20 ppb for ozone (National Center for Environmental Assessment, 2006; EPA, 2009).

Affected Populations

We used 2010 U.S. Census Bureau population estimates included in BenMAP. The affected population for each health endpoint was considered to be all members in the Pittsburgh MSA of the age group included in the primary study used to estimate the CR function. For example, the affected population for SLDs includes children

---

2 For percentage and incremental methods, BenMAP calculates either the percentage or increment necessary to reduce out-of-attainment values to the standard. To generate values using peak-shaving reduction, BenMAP truncates all monitor values at the standard. With quadratic reduction, large values are reduced proportionally more than small values while achieving the standard (Abt Associates, 2012). Although we ran scenarios with all reduction methods to generate a range of results, we first concentrated primarily on percentage and quadratic as the most-realistic reduction methods for the Pittsburgh MSA. EPA commonly employs both methods in benefit analyses, while the selection of the 2006 ozone standard was determined through modeling using the quadratic approach (EPA, 2008, p. 16467). Between these two reduction methods, it is not always clear which one would best simulate attainment in a given area (Rizzo, 2005; Hubbell et al., 2005). A suite of control strategies may be employed at any one time that could have proportional or quadratic effects. In addition, such factors as pollutant chemistry (e.g., formation, existence and extent of precursors), pollutant fate and transport characteristics, the presence and types of sources in the area, background concentrations of pollutants, and an area's topographical and meteorological characteristics can all act to influence or modify the process through which air pollution is reduced and attainment reached. In a comparative analysis of percentage and quadratic reductions, Rizzo (2006) determined that the methods did not vary greatly from each other at sites with a small range of ozone concentrations. In contrast, in areas with large differences between minimum and maximum ozone concentrations, the two methods diverged. However, in general, a percentage reduction better approximates control strategies that are broad, regionally focused, and expected to lower pollutant concentrations consistently throughout the area and over time. In contrast, quadratic reductions better reflect control strategies that might be more local in scope, target high emitters, or act on a temporary basis.

between 5 and 17 years old in the Pittsburgh MSA, while the affected population for WLDs includes adults between ages 18 and 64.

Economic Valuation

To estimate the economic benefits of improved health outcomes, we multiplied the estimated change in health outcomes by the economic value associated with each outcome. For most health endpoints, we used the default values in BenMAP. For the detailed WLD analysis, we instead valued a WLD using the daily median wage in the Pittsburgh MSA, taken from the Bureau of Labor Statistics for 2011 (eight times the hourly median wage of $16.45, or $131.60 per day) (Bureau of Labor Statistics, 2011a). For the detailed SLD estimates, we followed EPA methodology but updated the values using more-recent data. SLDs were valued by determining (1) the total number of single, married, and other (e.g., widowed) women in the workforce with children in 2009 and (2) the labor force participation rate of each category of women with children (U.S. Census Bureau, 2012a). These estimates were combined to generate the participation rate of women with children in the workforce in 2009 (71.7 percent). We then determined the median weekly wage among women 25 and older in 2010 ($704 per week) (Bureau of Labor Statistics, 2011b) and divided by 5 to obtain the median daily wage. The expected loss in wages due to a child missing a day of school is estimated as the probability that a mother is in the workforce multiplied by the daily wage she would lose if a working day was missed, which came out to $101 (Abt Associates, 2012).[3]

Limitations

There are several limitations and uncertainties inherent in our estimates of incidence changes from the health impact function and economic valuations. These generally lie in the following areas: air pollution exposure and health response parameters and economic valuations.

Air Pollution Exposure

One uncertainty in exposure estimation is found in the spatial interpolation method employed. Because we did not use modeling data to determine distributions of ozone and $PM_{2.5}$ across the Pittsburgh MSA, our approach calculates benefits based solely on monitor data. Monitor data cannot account for individual-level exposure or variations in exposure across time and space. The VNA approach uses a relatively simple inverse distance weighting in which the further a monitor is from a specified grid-cell point, the less weight is placed on its metrics. However, this approach does not

---

[3] Determining which parent would be more likely to stay home with a sick child is beyond the scope of our study. We therefore followed the standard EPA assumption that a mother will stay home with a sick child. Note that the overall median wage was approximately 11 percent higher than the female median wage in 2010, so our assumption may underestimate the cost of SLDs if a father stays at home instead.

take into account meteorology (temperature, humidity), terrain, precursor emissions, or other factors that an air quality model can incorporate. It is possible that our results do not capture the full range of benefits because numerous studies have shown that monitor data tend to underestimate personal exposures (Bell, 2006). However, without an adequate understanding of the spatial gradients in air pollution across the Pittsburgh MSA, it is difficult to determine whether monitors are under- or overestimating true exposures. In addition, the results of our analysis do not capture the uncertainty inherent in the air quality control scenarios. Standard deviations and percentile points around the benefits are determined through variability measures related to the CR functions and economic valuations.

Response Parameters and Economic Valuations

There are two levels of uncertainty associated with baseline incidence rates, CR functions, and economic valuations. The first level applies to the estimates themselves—how they were originally derived and the degree to which they represent the phenomena they are measuring. One particular challenge is that the SLD incidence data are based on all-cause absenteeism (for the Pittsburgh MSA data) or on medical leave and sickness absenteeism (for the Pittsburgh-only data). We were unable to identify a data source that estimated SLDs specifically associated with air quality–related respiratory illness. Therefore, our analysis likely overestimates the impact of reduced $PM_{2.5}$ on SLDs.

The second level of uncertainty applies to the degree to which the estimates are representative of the Pittsburgh MSA. For the detailed WLD and SLD analyses, where possible, we tried to use local-level data (e.g., SLD incidence, Pittsburgh MSA median wage data). Overall, if the Pittsburgh MSA differs in key ways from the populations that were used to derive the CR functions that would affect the exposure-response relationship, then the CR functions may not be applicable.

Finally, these estimates represent the mean or median of the population and may not adequately capture finer variations in response parameters. Certain subpopulations may be more sensitive to $PM_{2.5}$ or ozone effects and may thus show greater health gains due to air pollution reductions. We are unable to quantify or characterize subgroup effects in the present analysis.

Extrapolation of Effects of Nonattainment Status to the Pittsburgh Region

We drew on findings from national studies of nonattainment status to address the question: If Pittsburgh were in attainment with the NAAQS, what would be the effect on the number of local establishments, employment, and output? We extrapolated estimates from two studies that consider the effects of nonattainment status on industry outcomes at a national level to the Pittsburgh region, using local data on baseline values of establishments, employment, and output. These studies identify the effects of nonattainment status by comparing counties that are in attainment with those that are not in attainment, focusing on pollution-intensive industries.

In this section, we describe our methodology for these extrapolations and the associated limitations.

Number of Establishments

To estimate the effect of nonattainment status on the number of establishments, we drew on results from Henderson (1996). He compares changes in the number of establishments in five polluting industries in counties that are not in attainment for ozone with counties that are in attainment for ozone. Drawing on data from 1978 to 1987, he controls for county-specific characteristics that do not change over time and identifies the effect of nonattainment status by examining changes within individual counties over time. He finds that being in attainment for three or more years is associated with a 6- to 9-percent increase in the number of establishments in the organic chemicals, petroleum refining, plastic materials, and miscellaneous plastics industries; there is no statistically significant change in the number of establishments in the steel industry.

To extrapolate these effects to the Pittsburgh region, we collected data on the number of establishments in these industries in the Pittsburgh MSA from the 2010 County Business Patterns survey of the U.S. Census Bureau. We then multiplied the estimated effect for each industry by the number of establishments in that industry.

To estimate the associated change in payroll, we also multiplied the estimated change in the number of establishments by average payroll per establishment in that industry.[4] Average payroll per establishment was calculated by dividing, for the relevant industries, the total payroll value by the total number of establishments in the Pittsburgh MSA. Because payroll information was not available for the full set of industries under consideration, we based our payroll estimate data on information about the relevant industries for which data were available.[5]

Employment and Output

To estimate the effect of nonattainment status on employment, we used results from Greenstone (2002). Greenstone compares changes in employment, capital stock, and output (the value of shipments) from polluting industries in counties that are out of attainment with changes in counties that are in attainment for ozone, total suspended particulates (TSP), sulfur dioxide, or carbon monoxide. Drawing on data from 1967 to

---

[4] We note that payroll is perhaps more closely linked with output than with the number of establishments; however, the underlying study by Henderson focused on number of establishments, and we provide the payroll numbers only to provide a different sense of the magnitude of the effect.

[5] Because of data privacy issues, the census does not provide average payroll data for certain industries at the MSA level.

1987, Greenstone controls for plant-specific characteristics and identifies the effects of nonattainment status by examining changes within plants over time. In addition, he compares polluting industries and nonpolluting industries, which helps to control for county-specific trends.

We focused on the two criteria pollutants for which most of the Pittsburgh MSA is out of attainment: ozone and $PM_{2.5}$. Because the Greenstone (2002) study is based on years in which particulates were regulated as TSP, we assumed that the effect is the same for $PM_{2.5}$ (a subset of TSP). When controlling for plant-specific characteristics, Greenstone (2002) finds that ozone nonattainment status is associated with a 4.9-percent reduction in employment in a statistically significant manner. TSP nonattainment status is also associated with a 2.4-percent reduction in employment, while ozone and TSP nonattainment status are each associated with 3.2-percent reductions in output, although these results are not statistically significant.

We combined study results with U.S. Census Bureau estimates of employment in 2010 and output (measured as the value of shipments) in 2007, for industries covered in the study, in the Pittsburgh MSA. This provided us with a rough estimate of the relationship between being designated as out of attainment for ozone and $PM_{2.5}$ and employment and output in pollution-intensive industries (relative to non–pollution-intensive industries). We also estimated the effect on payroll in the same manner as described above for the Henderson (1996) study.

Limitations

We selected the Henderson (1996) and Greenstone (2002) studies for our extrapolation because they exploit the variation across counties and over time in attainment status to identify the effect of ozone and particulate matter pollution on local economic outcomes while controlling for other time-invariant, county-specific factors that might be correlated with nonattainment status and growth. However, there are limitations associated with the studies themselves and with the extrapolation to the Pittsburgh region.

First, because of the nature of the regressions in these studies, they are limited to examining pollution-intensive industries (and, in the case of Greenstone, 2002, the results are for pollution-intensive industries relative to non–pollution-intensive industries). To the extent that there are spillovers to non–pollution-intensive industries, these effects will not be captured. Second, both of these studies are based on national estimates; there are reasons that the national results may not apply to the Pittsburgh region. One potential reason is that the studies identify industries that are heavy polluters at the national level. To the extent that these industries have a larger or smaller share of major emitters in the Pittsburgh region than they have nationally, the effects may be larger or smaller. We examined the extent to which this could be a concern using EPA's Air Facility System database of permitted facilities. For the industries identified by Henderson (1996) and by Greenstone (2002) as major ozone sources, the ratio of major emitters to total permitted facilities for ozone precursors (NO_x and VOCs) is similar in the Pittsburgh MSA and nationally. However, for the industries identified by Greenstone (2002) as major $PM_{2.5}$ sources, the ratio of major emitters to total permitted facilities is higher in the Pittsburgh MSA (0.16) than nationally (0.1). This suggests that our estimates understate the extent of forgone employment or output as a result of Pittsburgh's nonattainment status.

Third, these studies are based on data from the 1970s and 1980s; a variety of factors may result in different effects of nonattainment status today, including differing regulations associated with nonattainment status, which specific industries are large emitters, and what types of pollution control methods are available. Fourth, the regions that are currently in nonattainment for $PM_{2.5}$ are the Liberty-Clairton and Pittsburgh–Beaver Valley regions, which together account for an area similar to the Pittsburgh MSA; however, the Pittsburgh–Beaver Valley region includes portions of Greene and Lawrence counties and excludes Fayette County and parts of Armstrong County. Given data availability constraints, we used employment and output data at the Pittsburgh MSA level.

Finally, in order to match the industries identified in the studies with employment and establishment data from the census, we had to match the older industry codes from the studies (Standard Industrial Classification [SIC] codes) with newer industry codes used by the census (North American Industrial Classification System [NAICS] codes). Preliminary matching between SIC and NAICS codes was performed using the crosswalks for 1987 SIC to 2002 NAICS and 2002 NAICS to 1987 SIC (U.S. Census Bureau, 2013). However, in many cases, the crosswalks left the correspondence unclear. Some SIC codes correspond to several NAICS codes. In addition, the crosswalks show correspondence at the six-digit NAICS code level; in some cases, a higher-level match was more appropriate. We manually adjusted the preliminary matches to select the best overall correspondence. In Appendix E, we provide a list of the SIC codes from the original studies and the NAICS codes with which we matched them.

CHAPTER THREE

Existing Evidence for Links Between Local Air Quality and Economic Growth

In this chapter, we lay out a conceptual framework describing the three key ways in which local air quality could influence local economic growth. This framework was largely based on our review of relevant literature but also informed by our stakeholder interviews. For each of these effects, we then summarize our review of the existing evidence from the literature. Appendix A provides a table that lists the main studies we included in our literature review, along with their key assumptions, limitations, and findings. In some areas in which substantial literature exists (particularly in the literature on air quality and health, for example), we do not attempt to provide a comprehensive list of studies but rather include several representative examples.

It is worth noting that our conception of economic growth reflects traditional economic measures (e.g., gross regional product). To the extent that we examine quality-of-life issues, we do so because they may affect worker (or firm) location choices and thus economic performance. However, other studies may use broader definitions of *economic growth* that include, for example, life satisfaction (see, among others, Luechinger, 2009).

We identified three main ways by which air quality could affect local economic growth:

- **Pathway 1: Health and related workforce issues and costs.** This effect considers the links from air quality to the health of the local population, and subsequently to effects on the health and productivity of the local workforce. Workforce productivity and health can affect business costs and productivity and, thus, local economic growth.
- **Pathway 2: Quality-of-life issues and location decisions.** Air quality may affect quality of life for residents, either directly or through health effects. In turn, quality of life may influence business and residential location decisions, thus affecting growth.[1]

---

[1] There are clearly overlapping elements between pathways 1 and 2. We separated them for the purposes of our analysis because the literature tends to focus either on health and workforce outcomes or on quality-of-life issues (which are often based on health). The two strands of literature for these pathways are quite distinct.

- **Pathway 3: Air quality regulations and business operations.** The stringency of national air quality regulations varies with local air quality. Therefore, local air quality indirectly influences business costs and location decisions via its effect on applicable regulations.

In the following sections, we discuss each effect in more detail and summarize the evidence from existing literature.

Links from Air Quality to Health and to Workforce Productivity

Poor air quality can adversely affect health in many ways (EPA, 1999, 2011a). Poor health may have immediate effects on the workforce through short-run outcomes, such as WLDs and SLDs, or may have long-run impacts via the size or productivity of the workforce. Workforce productivity, in turn, may affect economic growth directly or may be a factor in business location decisions (Figure 3.1).[2]

Air Quality and Health

An extensive body of evidence demonstrates the myriad effects of air pollution on health, including impacts on neurological, respiratory, cardiovascular, and reproductive systems, and associations with cancer and premature mortality. EPA is required to periodically review and update the NAAQS if the latest scientific research indicates that current standards are not adequately protective. As part of its review, the agency develops a criterion document or integrated science assessment, which summarizes the weight of evidence to date for various health outcomes associated with the criteria pollutant of interest (EPA, 2009, 2010, 2013a, 2013b). These documents contain a comprehensive review of the scientific literature and form the scientific basis for determining air standards.

In this section, we focus on two specific health outcomes that are particularly salient to current workforce productivity. First, air pollution can increase the number of days that workers stay home due to respiratory or other pollution-related illnesses (WLDs). Second, air pollution can increase the number of days that children miss school due to pollution-related illnesses (SLDs). SLDs can increase WLDs because parents may have to stay home to care for their sick children. In the long run, a higher rate of absenteeism from school may be linked with lower educational attainment and therefore with lower future worker productivity.

---

[2] A related way in which air quality could affect growth is through its potential impact on a city's or region's average health insurance costs, thus changing the costs borne by businesses that provide insurance for their workers and affecting business location decisions. However, we were unable to find any studies that examined the links between air quality–related health outcomes and health insurance costs.

Figure 3.1
Links from Air Quality to Health-Related Outcomes and to Workforce Productivity

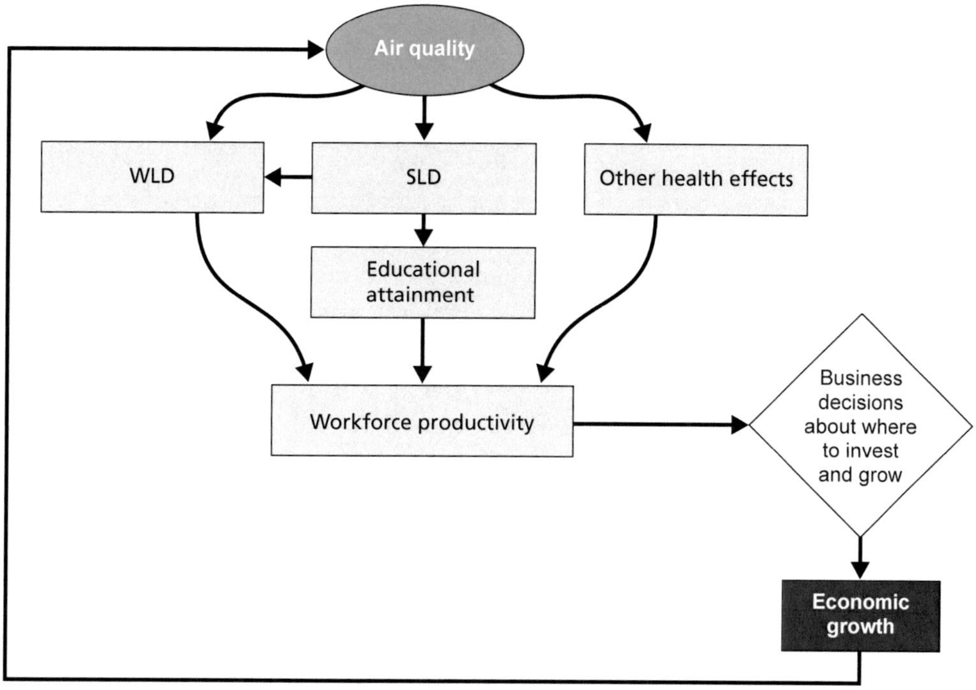

RAND *RR260-3.1*

Work-Loss Days

Several studies have documented an association between pollutants, particularly PM and ozone, and WLDs, restricted activity days, and the on-the-job productivity of outdoor workers.[3] The magnitude of the effect differs across pollutants, morbidity endpoints, and studies. For example, Crocker and Horst (1981) find that ozone reduces the productivity and earnings (by up to 2 percent, on average) of agricultural workers in Southern California. Hausman, Ostro, and Wise (1984) show that a one-standard-deviation increase in TSP is associated with a 10-percent increase in WLDs. Ostro (1987) confirms that increased PM concentrations are associated with more restricted-activity days and WLDs, although the effects vary across years in his study. Ostro and Rothschild (1989) find that PM increases both minor restrictions on activity and

[3] Because many workers spend their time indoors rather than outdoors, a growing literature also examines the relationship between indoor air quality and worker productivity. The literature in this area suggests that improving the indoor working environment may increase worker productivity (see, for example, Fisk, Black, and Brunner, 2011; Menzies et al., 1997; Milton, Glencross, and Walters, 2000; Wargocki et al., 2000; and Wyon, 2004). However, Wyon (2004) cautions that it is not yet clear which specific substances in indoor air cause productivity or sick-leave effects or through which mechanisms the effects occur. In addition, indoor and outdoor workers may face fundamentally different sets of air quality–related issues; in fact, outdoor airflow is often used as a means of *improving* indoor air quality.

WLDs but that ozone increases only minor restrictions on activity. More recently, Graff Zivin and Neidell (2012) find that a 10-ppb decrease in ozone is associated with a 5.5-percent increase in agricultural worker productivity in California.[4]

School-Loss Days

The association between low air quality and school absenteeism has been documented for certain pollutants. Exposure to ozone (Chen et al., 2000; Romieu et al., 1992; Gilliland et al., 2001) and carbon monoxide (Chen et al., 2000; Currie et al., 2007) is associated with school absences in children. For ozone, the magnitude of the effect may be quite large; for example, Chen et al. (2000) report that the daily absence rate would increase by 13 percent for every 50-ppb increase in ozone in the preceding two weeks; Romieu et al. (1992) find that preschool-age children exposed for two consecutive days to high ozone levels experience a 20-percent increase in the occurrence of respiratory illness–related school absence; and Gilliland et al. (2001) report that a 20-ppb increase in average daily ozone is associated with increases in school absences related to various illnesses ranging from 45 to 174 percent.

Studies that examine associations between PM less than 10 microns in diameter (PM_{10}) and school attendance tend to show mixed results. Ransom and Pope (1992) find significant and robust associations between grade-school absenteeism and PM_{10}; in their work, PM_{10} exposure is associated with a 40-percent increase in overall absences. In contrast, other studies report either weak or negative associations between PM_{10} and school absenteeism (Chen et al., 2000; Currie et al., 2007; Peters et al., 1997).

School absenteeism may affect the workforce in two ways: by requiring parents to take days off work to care for their children and by affecting long-term educational attainment (and thus the future workforce). There is some survey-based evidence of the relationship between childhood absence from school and parental WLDs. For example, a survey in Seattle finds that parents reported missing one day of work for every three days of school missed by children because of influenza (Neuzil, Hohlbein, and Zhu, 2002), while a survey of parental attitudes toward vaccination suggests that 53 percent of families reported experiencing adult WLDs in caring for sick children (Nettleman et al., 2001). These surveys are not specific to air pollution–related illnesses but do suggest that parents miss some workdays because of school absences.

There is considerable evidence linking school absences with poor educational attainment, psychological and behavioral problems, and future economic hardships. In a summary of the literature, Gottfried (2010) reports that school absenteeism has been associated with poor examination outcomes (Nichols, 2003; Roby, 2004), nonpromotion to higher grade levels (Neild and Balfanz, 2006), and dropping out (Rumberger

---

[4] There are also international studies on this topic. For example, Hanna and Oliva (2011) examine the closure of a refinery in Mexico City and show that a 1-percent reduction in SO_2 results in a 0.61-percent increase in hours worked. Hansen and Selte (2000) find that higher concentrations of PM_{10} are associated with more sick leaves in Oslo, while the relationship between concentrations of SO_2 and NO_2 and sick leaves is not clear.

and Thomas, 2000). In contrast, school attendance is related to higher grade-point averages and test scores (Gottfried, 2010). In addition, decreased school attendance is correlated with current and future risky behaviors, such as alcohol and drug use (Hallfors et al., 2002). Economically, students with lower school attendance records are more likely to face future financial hardships, such as unemployment (Broadhurst, May-Chahal, and Paton, 2005; Kane, 2006).

Although air pollution has been associated with school absences, and school absences have been associated with negative outcomes, the degree to which absenteeism *caused by air pollution* affects performance and potentially leads to other negative outcomes (such as behavioral problems) has not been adequately studied. Two studies assess school attendance and school performance in asthmatics, a group known to be vulnerable to air pollution effects. Silverstein et al. (2001) find that, although children with asthma experienced an average of two more days of absenteeism than children without asthma, there was no discernible difference in school performance as measured by reading, math, and language test scores, grade-point averages, grade promotion, or class rank of graduating students. Moonie et al. (2008) study an urban African American population and find no difference between students with asthma and those without asthma in test scores. However, the authors do find a significant inverse relationship between absenteeism and academic performance in all children.

In contrast, two studies hypothesize an effect of air pollution on academic performance. Zweig, Ham, and Avol (2009) examine the effects of PM_{10}, $PM_{2.5}$, NO_2, and ozone on math and reading test scores in California schoolchildren. After controlling for potential confounders, the authors find associations between higher levels of $PM_{2.5}$, PM_{10}, and NO_2 and lower math scores, with $PM_{2.5}$ showing the largest effects. $PM_{2.5}$ is also associated with lower reading test scores. Although the authors do not examine the means through which air pollution affects academic performance, they hypothesize four potential pathways: (1) school absenteeism due to air pollution–related illness; (2) attention problems caused by pollution-related illness; (3) fatigue caused by pollution-related illness; and (4) direct effects of air pollution on brain and cognitive development. Similarly, Mohai et al. (2011) examine the relationship between air pollution from industrial sources surrounding public schools in Michigan and children's academic achievement. The authors find that schools located in areas with the highest air pollution levels tend to have the lowest attendance rates, as well as the largest proportion of students failing state educational testing standards. These effects persist even after controlling for school location, spending per student, and school-level socioeconomic variables. However, the study does not account for individual-level socioeconomic characteristics, and the authors caution that the ecological design does not infer causality but points to the need for more research.

Air Quality–Related Health Outcomes and Growth

Next, we would ideally test whether air quality–related health effects influence economic growth. However, as discussed in Chapter One, there are factors that make it difficult to directly measure such an effect. Instead, impacts on growth are often inferred or assumed based on information about the impacts of air quality on morbidity and mortality. For example, EPA recently developed a *general equilibrium model*—which accounts for relationships between all sectors of the economy, including households, firms, and government—to examine the impacts of the 1990 Clean Air Act Amendments (Pub. L. 101-549) on national economic growth. In this model, reduced morbidity and premature mortality have a positive impact on long-run national gross domestic product (GDP) by providing more labor to the workforce (EPA, 2011a).[5] A strength of this type of model is that it does allow a projection of the impact of air quality improvements on GDP. However, a key weakness is that it requires strong assumptions about the structure of the economy and about how workers and firms behave.

Links from Air Quality to Quality of Life and Location Decisions

In this section, we consider the ways in which air quality could affect quality of life through its effect on health, on outdoor recreation,[6] or on the environment. As illustrated in Figure 3.2, quality-of-life considerations, in turn, may affect the choices that individuals make about where to live and that businesses make about where to locate.

There are studies that examine the relationship between quality-of-life considerations and individual or business location decisions (see, among others, Gottlieb, 1994; Porell, 1982; Salvesen and Renski, 2003). Our interviews with recruiters, site selection firms, and other businesses also confirmed qualitatively that quality of life is one factor among many that individuals and businesses consider when deciding where to locate. In this section, we do not attempt to summarize the literature on *all* quality-of-life

[5] Considering only costs, EPA (2011a) finds that the amendments reduced GDP by 0.52 percent in 2010 and 0.54 percent in 2020 compared with a scenario in which the amendments were not enacted. The agency incorporated labor force benefits (from reduced PM- and ozone-related medical expenditures and changes in workers' time endowment because of reduced PM- and ozone-related morbidity and PM-related premature mortality), as well as the costs of compliance. In this case, the agency found that the amendments are associated with a 0.21-percent reduction in GDP in 2010 but a 0.02-percent increase in GDP by 2020. The reason for this reversal is that the labor force effect is expected to grow more quickly than the compliance cost effect because mortality and morbidity benefits are cumulative over time. The findings from earlier general equilibrium models suggest similar results; when only costs of environmental regulations are considered, such regulations are associated with lower GDP (Jorgenson and Wilcoxen, 1990; Hazilla and Kopp, 1990; Jorgenson and Goettle, 2001); however, when both costs and labor force benefits are considered, these regulations are associated with higher long-run GDP (Jorgenson and Goettle, 2001).

[6] Outdoor recreation itself may create economic growth opportunities for firms in outdoor-related industries. We did not identify any literature that specifically addresses such opportunities.

Figure 3.2
Links from Air Quality to Quality of Life and Location Decisions

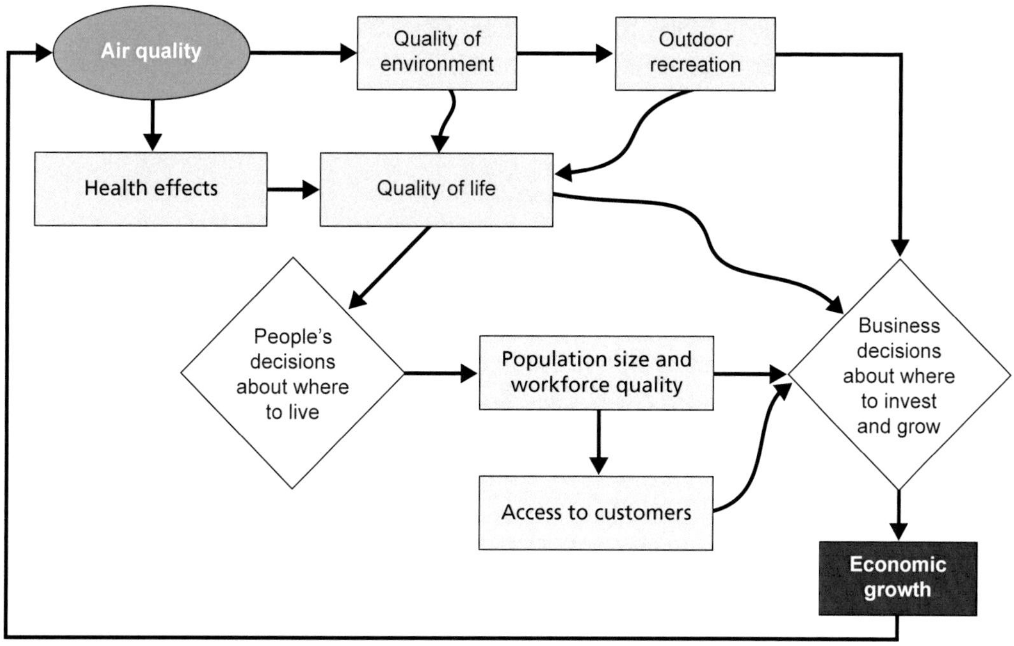

RAND *RR260-3.2*

factors and location decisions; rather, we focus on studies that specifically consider air quality and quality-of-life or location decisions.

Air Quality and Quality of Life

Several studies find that air quality is correlated with perceived quality of life (for studies using European populations, see, for example, Di Tella and MacCulloch, 2008; Luechinger, 2009, 2010; and Welsch, 2006). For the United States, Gabriel, Mattey, and Wascher (2003) assess the evolution in quality-of-life rankings by households from 1981 to 1990. Although, overall, rankings remained stable in most states, some showed substantial deterioration in estimated quality of life over the decade. Increased air pollution, as measured by ozone and carbon monoxide levels, is found to be correlated with decreased rankings (along with other factors, including reduced spending on infrastructure and increased traffic congestion). Similarly, Levinson (2009) finds that people who were surveyed about how happy they were typically reported lower levels of happiness when air pollution was worse than average local seasonal pollution.

We also searched for evidence on whether air quality could affect quality of life via its effect on recreation in urban settings.[7] Chapko and Solomon (1976) find that air pollution reduces attendance at some, but not all, urban attractions in New York City. More recently, Neidell (2006) finds that smog alerts in Southern California reduce attendance at two outdoor venues by approximately 10 percent. Neidell also documents potential substitution between outdoor activities and indoor activities on days when smog alerts are announced.

Air Quality and Location Decisions

Banzhaf and Walsh (2008) document that communities in California experiencing increases in the level of toxic air and water emissions (measured by the Toxics Release Inventory [TRI]) lose population, relative to other communities. Their evidence is consistent with the broader literature on air quality and housing prices, which finds that (controlling for other characteristics that would be expected to affect housing values) cleaner air is associated with higher housing prices. Smith and Huang (1995) conduct a review of the earlier literature and document that the median household would be willing to pay approximately $22 (in 1982–1984 dollars) for a 1-$\mu g/m^3$ reduction in TSP. More recently, Chay and Greenstone (2005) and Bayer, Keohane, and Timmins (2009) find larger effects; for example, the latter find that the median household would be willing to pay $149–185 (in 1982–1984 dollars) for a 1-$\mu g/m^3$ reduction in PM.

Although Banzhaf and Walsh (2008) find evidence that people do "vote with their feet" for cleaner air, they point out, "given constraints on mobility related to family, career, and other networks, residential responses to changes to public goods are most likely to occur within, rather than across, metropolitan areas."[8] In fact, one reason for the larger willingness to pay (WTP) identified by Bayer, Keohane, and Timmins (2009) is that these authors account for the fact that moving to a new city is costly.

We identified a few studies that examine the relationship between air quality and intercity or interstate migration. Cebula and Alexander (2006) find that states with fewer hazardous-waste sites and lower toxic chemical releases per person in 2000 had higher in-migration between 2000 and 2004, while Porell (1982) documents that states with lower levels of PM and SO_2 concentrations and fewer annual inversion days had higher in-migration rates between 1965 and 1970. Chay and Greenstone (2005) examine populations by county before and after the passage of the 1970 Clean Air Act

[7] The broader literature on the economic effects of air pollution on tourism focuses on ecotourism, haze and visibility in national parks, or the effects of acid rain on sensitive locations and structures that attract tourists. A more relevant tourism-related outcome for the Pittsburgh region may be links between air quality and convention-related tourism, but our search of the literature did not identify published studies on this topic.

[8] Their "communities" are defined as 0.5-mile-diameter circles in the vicinity of San Francisco and Los Angeles. They do not provide estimates for how much movement they see between these two metropolitan areas versus within an individual metropolitan area.

and provide some evidence that individuals "sort" into counties based on their preferences for clean air.

We also identified a few studies that examine the relationship between air or environmental quality and business location decisions. In a review of several studies, Gottlieb (1994) finds environmental quality to be the highest-ranking quality-of-life factor for high-technology firms and the third-highest-ranking quality-of-life factor for all firms. Informed by a national survey of research and development facilities and their employees, Malecki and Bradbury (1992) find that quality of education and environmental quality were the top two attributes that firms believed were most important to their employees. Hekman (1982) assesses business location decisions in North and South Carolina and Virginia from 1978 to 1982; business executives were asked to rank the importance of various business location factors and quality-of-life factors. Although quality-of-life factors were considered less important than economic factors, quality of air and water was one of the top-ranked quality-of-life factors, which also included the educational system, cost of living, housing, and personal taxes. Finally, in a survey of business executives in industrial firms (the president or chairman of the board), Foster (1977) finds that they considered the factor "clean environment" important on a personal level, as well as in the operation of the plant and to key personnel.

Local Air Quality, Air Quality Regulations, and Business Operations

Local air quality affects what types of air quality regulations are required in an area, most notably through EPA's categorization of areas as in *attainment* or *nonattainment* for one or more of the NAAQS. As illustrated in Figure 3.3, regulations in nonattainment areas are more stringent for firms that are considered major emitters of regulated pollutants, so these regulations can increase those companies' business costs and thus influence their location decisions. In this section, we examine the relationship between nonattainment status and a variety of firm outcomes.

Firm Location Decisions

Nonattainment status may affect the site selection decisions of certain firms. Here, we discuss three key reasons for this impact; Appendix C provides a summary of our discussions with site selection firms, including a general overview of the site selection process, as well as a qualitative discussion of the role played by air quality and air quality regulations.

First, new or expanding firms that emit significant amounts of a regulated pollutant (known as *major sources*) in a nonattainment area are required to install more-

Figure 3.3
Links from Local Air Quality to Air Quality Regulations and Business Operations

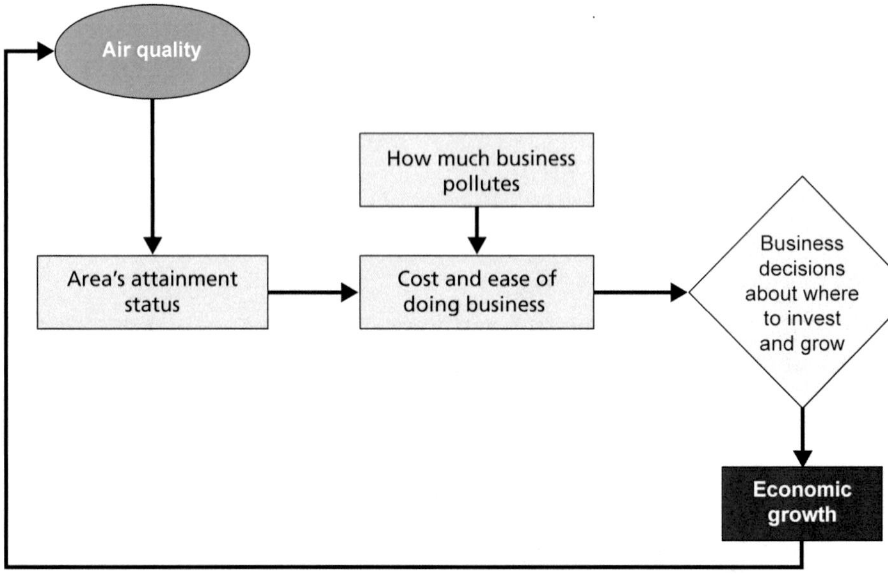

RAND *RR260-3.3*

stringent, and potentially more-expensive, pollution control technology.[9] Second, firms that are major sources of targeted pollutants in a nonattainment area have to obtain offsets—that is, decreases in that pollutant from other sources—in order to begin or significantly expand operations. Third, the permitting process for a major source in a nonattainment area is relatively lengthy.[10]

In the literature, the broader evidence on environmental regulations and business location is mixed, but county-level nonattainment status is associated with a deterrent effect on firm location. Jeppesen, List, and Folmer (2002) conduct a meta-analysis of 11 studies and argue that there have been two "waves" of studies on environmental regulations and business location decisions. The more recent wave of studies was conducted during the late 1990s, and many of these studies find that regulations do deter businesses from locating in an area. In contrast, the first wave took place during the late 1980s and early 1990s and typically provided little support for the hypothesis that regulations may deter firms from locating in the area. This meta-analysis suggests that the size and robustness of the impacts of environmental regulations on business location decisions depend on a variety of factors, including the estimation methods and the

[9] New or expanded major sources of the regulated criteria pollutants in nonattainment areas are required to install technology meeting the lowest achievable emission rate (LAER) standard, which does not take cost considerations into account, while those locating in attainment areas are required to install the Best Available Control Technology (BACT), which does take cost into account.

[10] These points are based on our discussions with local air quality regulators.

ways in which data are aggregated. Similarly, in their review of this literature, Brunnermeier and Levinson (2004) point out that, given the variety of methods, assumptions, and data sources used by each study, results may not be comparable across studies.

Perhaps most salient for the Pittsburgh region is the finding by Jeppesen, List, and Folmer (2002) that studies that use county-level attainment status, rather than other regulations that are measured at more-aggregated (for example, state) levels, are more likely to find a deterrent effect. One potential reason for this finding may be that businesses view different counties as more similar than different states in terms of factors that affect location; thus, county-level regulations may have more impact on location decisions than state-level regulations (Jeppesen and Folmer, 2001).

The results on nonattainment status are confirmed by more-recent studies, which indicate that new plants and relocating plants are less likely to locate in nonattainment areas than in attainment areas (for evidence from New York State, see List, McHone, and Millimet, 2003, and List, Millimet, Fredriksson, et al., 2003; for national evidence, see Morgan and Condliffe, 2009). Evidence from a national study suggests that polluting plants in nonattainment areas are more likely than polluting plants in attainment areas to shut down (Greenstone, List, and Syverson, 2012), although this is not supported by a study of plants in New York State, which finds no systematic association between nonattainment status and closures (List, Millimet, and McHone, 2004).

Cost and Productivity

Most of the literature on environmental regulations has documented that there are associated costs to regulated industries. EPA estimates that the national, annual, direct compliance costs of the Clean Air Act Amendments range from about $20 billion (in 2006 dollars) in 2000 to $65 billion in 2020 (EPA, 2011a). To some extent, cost projections should be cautiously interpreted because there is empirical evidence (Hammitt, 2000; Harrington, Morgenstern, and Nelson, 2000) that ex ante studies are more likely to overestimate regulatory costs (as well as the amount of pollution reduced).

Average, self-reported expenditure by manufacturing firms on pollution abatement capital expenditures (as collected by the U.S. Census Bureau) from 1990 to 1994 was 7 percent of new capital expenditures, although there was large variation across industries (for example, 1 percent in the printing and publishing industry and 42 percent in the petroleum and coal product industry) (Jeppesen, List, and Folmer, 2002). Between 1979 and 1988, in both attainment and nonattainment areas, firms with high emissions had higher self-reported air pollution abatement capital and operating expenditures than firms with low emissions. Firms with high emissions in nonattainment areas had higher pollution abatement expenditures than firms with high emissions in attainment areas, although the robustness of the effects varies across different types of pollutants, plant characteristics, and estimation methods (Becker, 2005).

A related issue is that regulations, by requiring that firms install pollution control equipment, perform additional activities, or modify their processes, may decrease firm productivity (the efficiency with which firms convert input into output). Many of the early studies on firm productivity and environmental regulations focused on the 1970s, when the United States manufacturing industry as a whole was undergoing a decline in productivity growth. Jaffe, Peterson, et al. (1995) summarize much of the work in this area and conclude that studies typically suggest a "modest adverse" effect; for the manufacturing sector as a whole, between 8 and 16 percent of the productivity growth slowdown could be attributed to environmental regulations, with substantially larger effects in certain industries, including the paper and electric utility industries. One potential reason for a decrease in productivity may be that more-stringent regulations discourage the creation of new sources or the modification of older sources, thus reducing the formation of new capital (Nelson, Tietenberg, and Donihue, 1993; List, Millimet, and McHone, 2004).

A recent study by Greenstone, List, and Syverson (2012) shows that productivity levels in surviving polluting plants in nonattainment areas are between 2 and 5 percent lower than productivity levels of polluting plants in attainment areas. Ozone nonattainment status is associated with the greatest difference in productivity, followed by TSP and SO_2; in contrast, carbon monoxide nonattainment status is associated with an increase in productivity. The effects also vary by industry; for ozone and carbon monoxide, effects are positive for some industries and negative for others.

Although much of the evidence suggests that environmental regulations decrease firm productivity, a few studies do not. For example, Berman and Bui (2001) find that more–heavily regulated refineries in the Los Angeles area underwent a temporary productivity decline during the 1980s but then increased their productivity between 1987 and 1992, even as productivity fell among less heavily regulated plants in other parts of the country. A study by Gray and Shadbegian (1995) shows that the relationship between pollution abatement expenditures and productivity depends on how the effects of environmental regulations are measured (for example, as pollution abatement expenditures, compliance status, enforcement activity, or emission levels) and on the type of analysis used (comparing productivity across firms at one point in time or within firms over time).

Some authors also argue that regulations can produce cost savings or productivity gains for regulated firms. Porter and van der Linde (1995) suggest that, in addition to improving environmental quality, environmental regulation could create benefits, including signaling companies about existing inefficiencies in their processes, raising corporate awareness about environmental pollution, reducing uncertainty about environmental investments, encouraging innovation, and leveling the playing field by not allowing companies that do not invest in the environment to prosper at the expense of companies that do.

A few studies document evidence for certain parts of this Porter hypothesis. Boyd and McClelland (1999) identify individual examples of win-win cases in which firms could reduce pollution, as well as input intensity. Lanoie, Patry, and Lajeunesse (2008) show that lagged investment in pollution control equipment is associated with increased productivity growth in certain industries. Three studies find evidence of links between environmental regulations and increased patenting of related environmental technologies (Lanjouw and Mody, 1996; Popp, 2006) and research and development (Jaffe and Palmer, 1997). However, Palmer, Oates, and Portney (1995) estimate that cost savings associated with the Porter hypothesis are two orders of magnitude smaller than pollution abatement and control expenditures.

Employment

Theoretically, it is not clear whether regulations would increase or decrease employment. Morgenstern, Pizer, and Shih (2002) decompose the potential effect of environmental regulations on employment in a regulated industry into three components: a cost effect because regulations may require more inputs for the same amount of output, thereby increasing employment; a factor-shift effect because activities required by environmental regulations may be more or less labor-intensive than other activities, which may increase or decrease employment; and a demand effect because environmental regulations may raise costs and thus output prices, lowering demand and therefore employment. In addition to the channels examined by these authors, regulations may cause some firms to shut down and thus decrease employment. There may also be spillover effects that reach beyond regulated businesses. Production (and thus employment) may shift to businesses with lower emissions within the same industry. Regulations could increase employment in industries in the pollution control and abatement sector. Changes in the regulated industry could also affect industries that provide supplies to the regulated industry or purchase goods or services from the regulated industry, thus leading to employment changes in the supplier or purchaser industries. However, in the long run, many economy-wide models assume that labor supply will equal labor demand, so that any changes in employment in pollution-intensive industries will be balanced by changes in employment in non–pollution-intensive industries.

Empirical studies typically examine the effects of environmental regulations on employment using three approaches. The first approach examines employment in the regulated industry. A key benefit of this approach is that it requires fewer assumptions about the way in which firms or individuals behave than the approaches discussed below. In addition, focusing on regulated firms allows researchers to rigorously control for many other factors that could affect employment.[11] This approach also allows researchers to focus on the industries that are most likely to be affected by regulations.

Empirical evidence on the impacts that environmental regulations can have on employment in a regulated industry is mixed. Three studies suggest a fairly small impact of various environmental regulations on employment. Duffy-Deno (1992)

[11] For example, regulated firms may be compared with nonregulated firms in the same county, thus controlling for county-specific effects.

finds a negative relationship between air pollution expenditures reported by firms from 1974 to 1982 and manufacturing employment within MSAs. However, the magnitude of the effect is small; a 10-percent increase in abatement expenditures is associated with less than a 1-percent decline in per capita manufacturing employment among Sunbelt MSAs. Berman and Bui (2001) examine the effects of stringent air quality regulations imposed on refineries in Southern California and compare those refineries with refineries in other parts of the United States; they conclude that, although the regulations raised costs among affected refineries, there was no statistically significant effect on employment. Morgenstern, Pizer, and Shih (2002) examine the relationship between environmental spending and employment in four polluting industries and estimate that, across all four industries, the 95-percent confidence interval of employment changes ranged from 2.8 jobs lost to 5.9 jobs gained for every $1 million of environmental expenditures and is slightly positive on average. They note that this accounts for anywhere from 14,000 jobs lost to 29,000 jobs gained, while 632,000 U.S. manufacturing jobs were lost during the time period they studied. This means that, at the most, environmental regulations accounted for 2 percent of manufacturing job losses during this time.

In contrast, one study documents a sizable impact of nonattainment status on local employment in regulated industries. Greenstone (2002) compares the change in employment in polluting industries (relative to nonpolluting industries) in areas that were designated as nonattainment (relative to attainment areas) between 1972 and 1987. He finds that nonattainment designations resulted in 590,000 job losses in polluting industries. This estimate is more than twice the number of job losses in manufacturing in nonattainment areas during this time, which implies that, in the absence of being designated as out of attainment, there would have been job gains rather than job losses in those areas. However, Greenstone also notes that some of the jobs lost in nonattainment areas likely shifted to attainment areas; therefore, job losses may be double-counted (because a loss in a nonattainment area may be a gain in an attainment area). If *all* such job losses are due to shifts to attainment areas, then there is no overall employment loss to the United States as a whole.

A drawback of focusing on regulated industries is the failure to account for how changes in the regulated industry may affect employment in other industries. The reason this may be important is illustrated by evidence from Henderson (1996). Although he does not conduct a formal study on employment effects, he provides some evidence that nonattainment designations affect regulated industries but may not reduce overall employment. Using data from 1978 to 1987, he shows that growth rates for establishments in pollution-intensive industries (and for the manufacturing sector as a whole) were lower in nonattainment areas than in attainment areas but that total employment growth was higher in nonattainment areas than in attainment areas.

The second approach for examining employment effects typically considers job changes in one or more industries outside the regulated sector. The most common approach is to consider potential job gains in the pollution control sector. These gains are often assumed to be short term and are reported in terms of job-years. A broader version of this approach examines changes in employment that may be induced in other industries that supply or purchase goods or services from the regulated or pollution control industries. For example, if regulations result in an increase in the price of electricity, industries that use a lot of electricity would bear increased costs. Similarly, suppliers to the pollution control sector may be expected to face higher demand for their goods or services.[12]

A third approach to estimating employment effects is to use a *general equilibrium model.* As discussed above, a key drawback of such models is that they require many assumptions about how firms and workers behave. In addition, many general equilibrium models assume that labor markets will "clear"—that is, in the long run, the supply of labor will equal the demand for labor. Therefore, there is no involuntary unemployment in such models. Rather, changes in employment levels occur because of changes in the size of the potential labor force and because households change the amount of time they allocate to labor versus leisure. For example, as discussed above, EPA (2011a) has developed a general equilibrium model of the United States for its analysis of the benefits and costs of the Clean Air Act Amendments. In its model, labor markets are assumed to clear, so the model does not provide insights about unemployment impacts. However, there are changes in employment levels because households may change the amount of labor they are willing to supply because of changes in real wages. There may also be changes in households' time availability due to changes in morbidity and mortality.

Taken together, these findings suggest that it may be less important to focus on how environmental regulations affect overall employment levels in the long run than to consider the short-run impacts on workers in affected industries. Recent work by Walker (2012) makes an important contribution in this area. He follows workers over time after the passage of the 1990 Clean Air Act Amendments, which designated many additional areas as being out of attainment. First, he finds that employment in polluting sectors in areas that became designated as out of attainment under the 1990 amendments fell to 10 percent below their initial levels during the following ten years (15 percent below employment in a comparison group of polluting sectors in attainment areas). Second, the wages of workers in polluting industries in newly designated

---

[12] An example of employment effects that extend beyond the regulated industry is provided by a recent EPA regulatory impact analysis of the proposed Mercury and Air Toxics Standards. EPA estimates that these standards would result in 46,000 one-time job-years gained in the pollution control sector. It also estimates that the rules will lead to 5,950 ongoing net job-years gained due to various changes in other sectors (3,890 job-years gained due to demand for pollution control inputs, 4,320 job-years gained due to pollution control operation, 2,500 job-years lost due to coal capacity retirements, 430 job-years lost due to changes in coal demand, and 670 job-years gained due to changes in natural gas demand) (EPA, 2011b). The report points out that these estimates do not include the effects of higher energy prices on other industries; they also do not quantify potential multiplier effects as changes in one sector ripple out to others.

nonattainment areas fell for approximately three years, then returned to preregulation levels within eight years after the changes. He estimates that the total net present value of lost wages ranges from approximately 20 to 25 percent of annual preregulation earnings and that these losses were largely borne by workers who separated from their plants, rather than by workers who remained at the same plants. Third, there may have been small spillover effects, yielding a slight wage drop (of less than 1 percent) in non-regulated industries in nonattainment areas. Finally, nonattainment status increased the probability that a worker moved to a different industry. Walker notes that it is more likely that a worker moved to a different industry in the same county, but some workers also move to different counties.

In the next chapter, we extrapolate several results from our review of the literature to Pittsburgh and discuss the extent to which the results may or may not be applicable locally.

CHAPTER FOUR

Extrapolating Existing Evidence to Pittsburgh

In this chapter, we extrapolate three sets of results from the existing literature to the Pittsburgh region. First, we examine the impact of attaining the NAAQS for $PM_{2.5}$ and ozone on key health outcomes, specifically acute bronchitis, acute myocardial infarction, asthma exacerbation, chronic bronchitis, emergency-room visits, hospital admissions, mortality, respiratory symptoms, and WLDs.[1] This analysis is based on results from nationwide studies that are used in the modeling software and on data that are for the region as a whole. Second, we conduct a more detailed analysis of the potential impact that attaining the NAAQS for ozone and $PM_{2.5}$ could have on two outcomes that may be particularly salient to local businesses: WLDs and SLDs. In this case, we begin with the default assumptions and results provided in the software we use, but we supplement this analysis by using regional or Pittsburgh-specific data whenever possible. Third, we extrapolate results from two nationwide studies to examine the potential impact of the Pittsburgh region's nonattainment status on establishments, employment, and output in pollution-intensive industries.

Analysis of Key Health Endpoints

We estimated the effects that reducing $PM_{2.5}$ and ozone concentrations in the Pittsburgh MSA from 2012 levels to the current standards could have on key health outcomes. The initial set of analyses was carried out using health incidence data that were not specific to the Pittsburgh region.

Table 4.1 presents the results of our analyses for ten health endpoints for $PM_{2.5}$ reductions. We assumed that Pittsburgh would first meet the annual mean standard and then take additional steps to achieve the daily maximum standard under a percentage reduction approach. The "Incidence Mean" column presents the estimate of avoided incidences for each health endpoint (shown in the "Endpoint" column). These estimates reflect the number of cases that would be avoided if Pittsburgh were to come

[1] Note that WLDs can be seen as an effect of health outcomes rather than an outcome per se, but we use this term the way it is used in the literature.

into attainment. The "Valuation" column shows the value (economic benefit) associated with each set of avoided incidences.

Because these estimates were based on summing up avoided incidences due to meeting the yearly and then the daily standards, we do not provide a measure of the associated uncertainty (i.e., a standard deviation) for the totals. However, Appendix D presents the estimated avoided incidences for the yearly and daily standards separately, including the standard deviations associated with each estimate.

The last row of Table 4.1 presents the total estimated value associated with the improvement in each of these health endpoints. Note that the total valuation is not equal to the sum of the individual valuations because the overall valuation was derived using simulation methods.[2]

Table 4.1
Annual Effect That Meeting the New $PM_{2.5}$ Standard Could Have on Key Health Endpoints in the Pittsburgh Metropolitan Statistical Area

Endpoint	Incidence Mean (number of avoided cases)	Valuation ($ thousands)
Acute bronchitis	72	27
Acute myocardial infarction	9	446
Asthma exacerbation	1,526	238
Chronic bronchitis	42	6,405
Emergency-room visits, respiratory	38	10
Hospital admissions, cardiovascular	16	414
Hospital admissions, respiratory	18	402
Adult mortality	89	486,185
Upper-respiratory symptoms	1,323	35
WLDs	7,243	857
Total		487,793

SOURCE: Authors' calculations using EPA's BenMAP software, with ambient air quality values updated to reflect 2012 concentrations in the Pittsburgh MSA.

NOTE: The total valuation is based on a Monte Carlo simulation of the underlying results for each endpoint and is therefore not equal to the sum of the individual valuations. The selection of endpoints relies on EPA's selection of epidemiological studies available in BenMAP.

2 Specifically, Monte Carlo simulation methods were used—5,000 draws were specified where, at each iteration, a value was chosen at random from the distribution of results and used to determine sums.

For $PM_{2.5}$, meeting the current NAAQS would be associated with a value of approximately $488 million in the Pittsburgh MSA, with most of the value coming from a reduction in expected premature adult mortality.

Table 4.2 presents similar results for ozone. The means and standard deviations of the number of avoided incidences are shown in the "Incidence" columns, while the associated values and their standard deviations are shown in the "Valuation" columns. The last row of Table 4.2 presents the total estimated value associated with the improvement in each of these health endpoints. As with $PM_{2.5}$, the total value is based on simulation methods and is therefore is not equal to the sum of the individual values. We estimate the total value associated with meeting the ozone NAAQS in the Pittsburgh MSA to be approximately $128 million.

Detailed Analysis of Work-Loss and School-Loss Days

As discussed in Chapter Two, we also performed a more detailed examination of the effects that reducing $PM_{2.5}$ could have on WLDs and the effects that reducing

Table 4.2
Annual Effect That Meeting the Ozone Standard Could Have on Key Health Endpoints in the Pittsburgh Metropolitan Statistical Area

	Incidence		Valuation ($ thousands)	
Endpoint	Number of Avoided Cases	Standard Deviation	Value	Standard Deviation
Emergency-room visits, respiratory	14	11	5	4
Hospital admissions, respiratory	26	18	832	557
Mortality	18	4	128,267	62,739
SLDs	5,600	1,666	566	168
Total			127,635	60,366

SOURCE: Authors' calculations using EPA's BenMAP software, with ambient air quality values updated to reflect 2012 concentrations in the Pittsburgh MSA.

NOTE: The total valuation is based on a Monte Carlo simulation of the underlying results for each endpoint and is therefore not equal to the sum of the individual valuations. The selection of endpoints relies on EPA's selection of epidemiological studies available in BenMAP.

ozone could have on SLDs because these two endpoints may be particularly salient for employers in the Pittsburgh area today.[3]

Table 4.3 presents results for the effect that meeting the new $PM_{2.5}$ standard could have on WLDs. This detailed analysis explores the sensitivity of the baseline results to varying the incidence rate (using the rates from large MSAs, from the Midwest, and from the Northeast). Using these incidence rates increases our estimate of the magnitude of the effect on WLDs substantially compared with using national-level WLD incidence rates (see Table 4.1). We find that reductions in $PM_{2.5}$ are associated with approximately 13,000 to 15,000 fewer WLDs per year. Given a median wage rate of $131.60 per day for the Pittsburgh MSA, this translates into a value between $1.7 million and $1.9 million per year.

For ozone, we estimated the effects of meeting the NAAQS using two sets of Pittsburgh-specific SLD baseline incidence rates and varying background ozone concentrations. Table 4.4 presents results based on all-cause incidence rates for the Pittsburgh MSA. In this case, we estimated that meeting the NAAQS is associated with approximately 6,700 to 10,500 fewer SLDs per year, depending on background concentration. Using standard assumptions about parents taking time off work to care for their children, this translates into a value of approximately $680,000 to $1 million per year. These values may be biased upward because the baseline incidence rate depends on all causes of absenteeism, not just absenteeism related to respiratory illness.

Table 4.5 presents results using the incidence rate from the City of Pittsburgh for absenteeism due to medical leave or sickness. We found that meeting the NAAQS is

Table 4.3
Detailed Results for the Effect That Meeting the Yearly and Daily $PM_{2.5}$ Standards Could Have on Work-Loss Days

	WLDs		
Incidence Type	**Baseline**	**Avoided**	**Valuation of Avoided ($ thousands)**
Large MSA	5,951,347	13,174	1,734
Midwest	5,962,042	13,198	1,737
Northeast	6,684,284	14,797	1,947

NOTE: We assumed that the Pittsburgh MSA would meet the annual standard first and then employ strategies to meet the daily standard.

[3] We did not examine the effects of ozone on WLDs or of $PM_{2.5}$ on SLDs because CR functions for these pathways are not included in EPA's BenMAP software. As discussed in Chapter Two, EPA typically selects studies based on a variety of considerations, including study design and location, characteristics of study populations, and whether studies were peer-reviewed.

Table 4.4
Detailed Results for the Effect That Meeting the Ozone Standard Could Have on School-Loss Days: All-Cause Incidence Rate

Background Level[a] (ppb)	Hourly Background Level[b] (ppb)	SLDs Avoided (baseline SLDs = 26,983,366) Number	Standard Deviation	Valuation ($ thousands) Amount	Standard Deviation
40	0	6,724	2,000	679	202
20	0	10,455	3,110	1,056	313
40	40	6,738	2,004	681	202
20	20	10,465	3,113	1,057	314

NOTE: Scenarios consisted of the Pittsburgh region meeting a standard of 75 ppb (fourth-highest maximum value at or below 75 ppb).

[a] *Background level* refers to the assumed background concentration of ozone specified for the attainment metric (in this case, fourth-highest daily maximum eight-hour average).

[b] *Hourly background level* is the assumed background for hourly ozone values.

Table 4.5
Detailed Results for the Effect That Meeting the Ozone Standard Could Have on School-Loss Days: Public School Medical Leave and Sickness Incidence Rate

Background Level (ppb)	Hourly Background Level (ppb)	SLDs Avoided (baseline SLDs = 17,260,752) Number	Standard Deviation	Valuation ($ thousands) Amount	Standard Deviation
40	0	4,301	1,280	434	129
20	0	6,688	1,990	676	200
40	40	4,310	1,282	435	129
20	20	6,694	1,992	676	201

NOTE: Scenarios consisted of the Pittsburgh region meeting a standard of 75 ppb (fourth-highest maximum value at or below 75 ppb).

associated with approximately 4,300 to 6,700 fewer SLDs per year. This translates into a reduction in WLDs valued at approximately $435,000 to $675,000 per year.

These results are subject to some uncertainties and limitations, which were discussed in Chapter Two. We view these figures not as a basis for policymaking but rather as a starting point for discussion about air quality in the Pittsburgh region.

Nonattainment Status and Industry Outcomes

Establishments

As discussed in detail in Chapter Two, we extrapolated results from Henderson (1996) to examine the effect that nonattainment status could have on the number of establishments in five pollution-intensive industries in Pittsburgh.

Table 4.6 presents results. Henderson's estimated effect on the number of establishments in each industry is shown in the first "Value" column, with associated 90-percent confidence intervals in the first "90% Confidence Interval" column. Because his dependent variable is the log of the number of establishments, the coefficients can be interpreted as the percentage change in the number of establishments associated with being in attainment for ozone for three or more years. For four out of five industries, the effects of being in attainment are positively associated with number of establishments, with mean effect sizes ranging from 6 percent to 9 percent. The results for each of these industries are statistically significant at the 10-percent level. For the fifth industry, steel, attainment status is negatively associated with the number of industries, but the result is not statistically distinguishable from zero.

The "Number of Establishments in Relevant Industries in the Pittsburgh MSA" column shows the number of establishments in each of these five industries in the Pitts-

Table 4.6
Estimated Effect That Being in Attainment for Ozone for Three or More Years Could Have on the Number of Establishments in the Pittsburgh Metropolitan Statistical Area

	Henderson's Estimation of Effect		Number of Establishments in Relevant Industries in the Pittsburgh MSA	Estimated Effect of Being in Attainment for Ozone on the Number of Pittsburgh MSA Establishments	
Industry	Value	90% Confidence Interval		Value	90% Confidence Interval
Industrial organic	0.091	[0.04, 0.14]	6	0.55	[0.26, 0.83]
Petroleum refining	0.065	[0.002, 0.13]	3	0.20	[0.007, 0.38]
Plastic materials	0.072	[0.021, 0.12]	13	0.94	[0.27, 1.60]
Miscellaneous plastics	0.081	[0.05, 0.11]	85	6.89	[4.23, 9.54]
Steel	−0.003	[−0.046, 0.04]	46	—[a]	—[a]
Overall	Not applicable	Not applicable	153	8.6	Not applicable

SOURCE: Estimated effects and associated confidence intervals are based on Henderson (1996), Table 4; numbers of establishments are from the 2010 County Business Patterns survey by the U.S. Census Bureau (2012b).

[a] Not provided because the parameter estimate is statistically indistinguishable from zero.

burgh region in 2010. In the "Estimated Effect of Being in Attainment for Ozone on the Number of Pittsburgh MSA Establishments" column, we extrapolate Henderson's results to the Pittsburgh region by multiplying the average effect ("Henderson's Estimation of Effect") by the number of establishments in the Pittsburgh region ("Number of Establishments in Relevant Industries in the Pittsburgh MSA"). The second "90% Confidence Interval" column presents the 90-percent confidence intervals associated with these extrapolations.

Extrapolating the Henderson results to Pittsburgh suggests that achieving attainment status in the Pittsburgh region would be associated with a small increase in the number of establishments in three industries (industrial organic, petroleum refining, and plastic materials) and an increase of nearly seven establishments in one industry (miscellaneous plastics). The reason that the effect is largest in miscellaneous plastics is because of the large number (85) of existing establishments in this industry currently in the MSA. Adding up all of the effects suggests that being in attainment would be associated with approximately eight more establishments in the Pittsburgh region.

Although we cannot place an exact value on these eight establishments, we gathered available data on average payroll per establishment in existing establishments in a subset of these industries (plastic materials, miscellaneous plastics, and steel) in the Pittsburgh region. The average payroll per establishment was estimated to be \$6.316 million per year. Multiplying average payroll per establishment by eight implies that ozone attainment status would be associated with payroll gains of \$50.5 million.

Employment and Output

We then extrapolated Greenstone's (2002) results on nonattainment status, employment, and output to the Pittsburgh region, as described in Chapter Two.

Table 4.7 presents results for employment. Greenstone's estimated percentage change in employment associated with nonattainment status for each pollutant is shown in the first "Value" column, with associated 90-percent confidence intervals in the "90% Confidence Interval" column. The effect of being out of attainment for ozone is 4.9 percent lower employment in pollution-intensive industries. The result is statistically significant at the 10-percent level. The effect of being out of attainment for TSP is 2.4 percent lower employment in pollution-intensive industries, but the result is not statistically significant.

The "Employment in Relevant Industries in the Pittsburgh MSA" column shows employment in the ozone-intensive and TSP-intensive industries in Pittsburgh in 2010. In the "Estimated Change in Employment in Regulated Industries in the Pittsburgh MSA from Being Designated as Out of Attainment" column, we extrapolate Greenstone's results to Pittsburgh by multiplying the average effect ("Greenstone's Estimation of Effect") by employment in Pittsburgh ("Employment in Relevant Industries in the Pittsburgh MSA"). The second "90% Confidence Interval" column presents the 90-percent confidence intervals associated with these extrapolations. Being designated

Table 4.7
Estimated Effect That Being Out of Attainment Could Have on Employment in the Pittsburgh Metropolitan Statistical Area

Pollutant	Greenstone's Estimation of Effect: Value	Greenstone's Estimation of Effect: 90% Confidence Interval	Employment in Relevant Industries in the Pittsburgh MSA	Estimated Change in Employment in Regulated Industries in the Pittsburgh MSA from Being Designated as Out of Attainment: Value	Estimated Change in Employment in Regulated Industries in the Pittsburgh MSA from Being Designated as Out of Attainment: 90% Confidence Interval
Ozone	−0.049	[−0.074, −0.024]	Lower: 39,055 Upper: 39,721	Lower: −1,914 Upper: −1,946	[−2,877, −950] [−2,926, −966]
TSP	−0.024	[−0.063, 0.015]	17,218	−413	[−1,093, 267]

SOURCE: Estimated effects and associated confidence intervals are based on Greenstone (2002), Table 5, Column 4. Numbers of employees are from the 2010 County Business Patterns survey of the U.S. Census Bureau (2012b).

NOTE: Lower and upper values are provided for ozone because the census provided only a range of employment for several industries.

as out of attainment for ozone is associated with approximately 1,900 fewer jobs,[4] while being designated as out of attainment for TSP is associated with about 400 fewer jobs.

As with establishments, we cannot place an exact value on the employment effects. We gathered available data on average payroll per employee in existing establishments in a subset of these industries (printing; rubber and plastic; fabricated metals; a subset of the motor vehicle industry; lumber and wood; stone, clay, glass, and concrete; and iron and steel) in the Pittsburgh MSA. The average payroll per employee was estimated to be $50,000 per year for pollution-intensive industries in ozone and $58,000 per year for pollution-intensive industries for TSP. Multiplying average payroll per employee by the job-loss estimates implies that ozone nonattainment status is associated with payroll losses of approximately $96 million. Similarly, TSP nonattainment status is associated with payroll losses of $24 million.

Table 4.8 presents results for output. Greenstone's estimated percentage change in output associated with nonattainment status for each pollutant is shown in the first "Value" column, with associated 90-percent confidence intervals in the first "90% Confidence Interval" column. The effect of being out of attainment is the same (3.2 percent lower output in pollution-intensive industries) for ozone and TSP, but neither result is statistically significant at the 10-percent level.

The "Value of Shipments in Relevant Industries in the Pittsburgh MSA" column shows output in the ozone-intensive and TSP-intensive industries in Pittsburgh in 2010. Complete output (shipment) data were available for only three out of nine industries

[4] For several industries that emit ozone precursors (organic chemicals, motor vehicles, and petroleum refining industries), the census provided only a range of employment. Therefore, we show results based on employment at the lower and upper ends of this range.

Table 4.8
Estimated Effect That Being Out of Attainment Could Have on the Value of Output in the Pittsburgh Metropolitan Statistical Area

Pollutant	Greenstone's Estimation of Effect: Value	Greenstone's Estimation of Effect: 90% Confidence Interval	Value of Shipments in Relevant Industries in the Pittsburgh MSA ($ billions)	Estimated Change in Output from Regulated Industries in the Pittsburgh MSA from Being Designated as Out of Attainment ($ millions): Value	Estimated Change in Output from Regulated Industries in the Pittsburgh MSA from Being Designated as Out of Attainment ($ millions): 90% Confidence Interval
Ozone	−0.032	[−0.071, 0.007]	7.155[a]	−229	[−511, 54]
TSP	−0.032	[−0.088, 0.024]	1.787[b]	−57	[−157, 43]

SOURCE: Estimated effects and associated confidence intervals are from Greenstone (2002), Table 6, Column 4. Values of shipments are from the 2007 Economic Census by the U.S. Census Bureau (2012c).

[a] Because of the narrow definition of certain industries, complete shipment data were available for only three out of nine industries that are classified as pollution-intensive for ozone, while partial shipment data were available for an additional two industries.

[b] Because of the narrow definition of certain industries, complete shipment data were available for only one out of four industries that are classified as pollution-intensive for TSP, while partial shipment data were available for an additional two industries.

that are classified as pollution-intensive for ozone and for one out of four industries that are classified as pollution-intensive for TSP; partial output data were available for an additional two industries in each category. Therefore, the output values can be considered lower bounds for the Pittsburgh MSA. In the "Estimated Change in Output from Regulated Industries in the Pittsburgh MSA from Being Designated as Out of Attainment" column, we extrapolate Greenstone's results to Pittsburgh by multiplying the average effect ("Greenstone's Estimation of Effect") by employment in Pittsburgh ("Value of Shipments in Relevant Industries in the Pittsburgh MSA"). The second "90% Confidence Interval" column presents the 90-percent confidence intervals associated with these extrapolations. Being designated as out of attainment for ozone and TSP is associated with $229 million and $57 million less, respectively, in output from these industries.

The limitations of these extrapolations were discussed in detail in Chapter Two. Our results should be interpreted as starting points for a discussion of potential effects in the Pittsburgh region for several reasons, most notably that they are based on impact estimates extrapolated from national data from a different time period and based on somewhat different definitions of *particulate pollution*. These results point to impacts on regulated industries in nonattainment versus attainment areas (and, in the case of the employment and output estimates, the estimates are relative to nonregulated industries). This is particularly important in the context of the employment results because displaced workers from regulated industries are likely to shift to other industries in the long run. As discussed in Chapter Three, a study of the 1990 Clean Air Act Amendments finds that workers who are displaced because of regulations are most likely to move to other industries within the same county but may also switch counties (Walker, 2012). To the extent that this national evidence holds true in the Pittsburgh region, it suggests that many (but not all) displaced workers are likely to stay in the metropolitan region. For workers who stay within the seven-county region, the transitional costs, rather than employment numbers per se, may be a better measure of the impact that nonattainment status can have on the local labor market.

CHAPTER FIVE

Conclusions

In this study, we examined three ways in which local air quality may influence local economic growth. We assessed the evidence for each effect, based on a review of the existing literature. We then extrapolated results from selected studies to the Pittsburgh region, to provide a sense of the economic value associated with achieving the NAAQS. Our estimates are based largely on national studies and should thus be seen as a starting point for a discussion of air quality and growth in the Pittsburgh region.

For pathway 1 (health and related workforce issues and costs), we estimated the economic value associated with improved health if the Pittsburgh region were to come into compliance with the ozone and $PM_{2.5}$ NAAQS. We estimated that reducing $PM_{2.5}$ concentrations from 2012 levels to the current NAAQS would be associated with a value of approximately $488 million, while reducing ozone concentrations from 2012 levels to the current NAAQS would be associated with a value of approximately $128 million. These values are driven primarily by reduced premature mortality.

We then performed a more detailed examination of the value associated with two health endpoints that may be particularly salient for employers because of their impacts on workforce productivity: WLDs and SLDs. For WLDs, we tested the sensitivity of our findings to different baseline incidence rates. We found that using more-specific incidence rates—for large MSAs, the Midwest, and the Northeast—increases our estimate of the magnitude of the effect on WLDs substantially compared with using national-level WLD incidence rates. For SLDs, which affect workforce productivity indirectly through parental absences from work, we used different assumptions about pollution reductions, and we incorporated Pittsburgh-specific data about baseline incidence rates. When we used Pittsburgh-specific baseline incidence rates, the results confirmed our findings from the baseline analysis using national rates.

For pathway 3, we extrapolated results from selected studies to estimate the effects of the Pittsburgh region's nonattainment status on local industries. We found that being in attainment with the NAAQS would be associated with approximately eight more establishments in the Pittsburgh region. Meanwhile, being in attainment with ozone and $PM_{2.5}$ standards would be associated with approximately 1,900 and 400 more jobs, respectively, and with $229 million and $57 million more output from regulated industries, respectively. Table 5.1 summarizes the benefits that we were able to quantify for Pittsburgh.

Our analysis is subject to certain limitations. In extrapolating results from national studies to Pittsburgh, we assumed that the relationship between air quality or air quality regulations and the metrics we considered could be extrapolated to a different area. This approach is consistent with way in which health benefit estimates are typically constructed (EPA, 2011a).

We also note that coming into compliance with the NAAQS entails costs on regulated industries. Estimating the costs of coming into compliance is outside the scope of our study; because we do not conduct a cost-benefit analysis, our aim is not to make specific policy recommendations. Instead, our goal in this study was to highlight some of the links between improved air quality and local growth. Discussions of air quality improvements often focus on health outcomes (on the benefit side) and direct costs (on the cost side). One of our aims was to highlight issues, including impacts on workforce productivity, business location decisions, and individual relocation decisions, that are not typically part of these discussions. Our work may also help to encourage a dialogue among policymakers, local organizations, and others interested in air quality and local growth in the Pittsburgh region and elsewhere.

Our findings suggest that local policymakers and others concerned with improving air quality in Pittsburgh may find it worthwhile to consider several points. First, the economic value associated with the health benefits of meeting the NAAQS in the Pittsburgh region is substantial and includes immediate benefits to local businesses in the form of reduced WLDs. Second, regulated industries face costs associated with improving air quality; however, our analysis suggests that, once national standards are met, businesses in those regulated industries may have an easier time locating and growing in the Pittsburgh region.

Table 5.1
Summary of Ways in Which Local Air Quality Influences Local Economic Growth

Effect	Summary	Relevance for Pittsburgh
Pathway 1: Health and workforce issues	Meeting NAAQS for ozone and $PM_{2.5}$ can reduce incidences of various health outcomes, such as premature mortality, emergency-room visits, and WLDs.	Annual benefit of $128 million for reducing ozone from 2012 levels to the NAAQS Annual benefit of $488 million for reducing $PM_{2.5}$ from 2012 levels to the NAAQS
Pathway 3: Activity in regulated industries	Coming into attainment with the NAAQS can make it easier for regulated industries to locate and operate locally in the long run.	Being in attainment with the ozone standard is associated with eight more establishments, 1,900 more jobs, and $229 million more output in regulated industries. Being in attainment with the $PM_{2.5}$ standard is associated with 400 more jobs and $57 million more in output from regulated industries.

Third, we found suggestive evidence that people do "vote with their feet" to live in places with cleaner air, particularly when it comes to local relocations. Although there is less empirical evidence on how air quality affects intercity migration decisions, our stakeholder interviews offered anecdotal evidence that recruiters use all possible tools when convincing potential employees to move to a particular city. The fact that Pittsburgh does not meet national air quality standards thus removes one potential tool from recruiters' toolkits. Encouraging local human resource departments in Pittsburgh firms to gather information from applicants about what factors played a role in their decisions to accept or reject an offered job, or using recruiting or survey data to examine the reasons that candidates from other parts of the country would or would not be willing to consider taking a job in Pittsburgh, could be important next steps in understanding the impacts of Pittsburgh's air quality on its potential to attract future residents.

APPENDIX A

Summary of Included Literature

Tables A.1 through A.7 summarize the literature we reviewed for this study.

Table A.1
Literature on Work-Loss Days

Author and Year Published	Study Date and Location	Key Pollutant or Regulation	Key Outcome	Main Methods, Assumptions, and Types of Evidence	Main Findings
Crocker and Horst, 1981	1973–1974, California	Ozone	Daily earnings of agricultural citrus pickers	Cross-sectional regression model of earnings on ozone concentrations and other factors	Required compensation to pickers for ozone concentrations ranges from 0 to 7.4% of earnings in the absence of air pollution (mean of 2.2%).
Graff Zivin and Neidell, 2012	2009–2010, California	Ozone	Worker productivity	Longitudinal regressions (including fixed-effect specifications) of worker productivity on daily ozone concentration	10-ppb decrease in ozone is associated with a 5.5% increase in worker productivity.
Hausman, Ostro, and Wise, 1984	1976, United States	TSP	WLDs	Cross-sectional count model of relationship between lost workdays and TSP	One-standard-deviation increase in TSP is associated with a 10% increase in WLDs.
Ostro, 1987	1976–1981, United States	$PM_{2.5}$	WLDs, restricted-activity days, respiratory restricted-activity days	Cross-sectional count model of the relationship between the outcomes and $PM_{2.5}$	$PM_{2.5}$ is positively associated with WLDs, restricted-activity days, and respiratory restricted activity in the majority of years in the sample.

Table A.2
Literature on School-Loss Days

Author and Year Published	Study Date and Location	Key Pollutant or Regulation	Key Outcome	Main Methods, Assumptions, and Types of Evidence	Main Findings
Chen et al., 2000	1996–1998, Nevada	PM_{10}, ozone, carbon monoxide	School absenteeism	Autoregression of percentage absenteeism on 24-hour PM_{10}, 1-hour maximum carbon monoxide, and 1-hour maximum ozone with control for potential confounding factors	For every 1-ppm and 50-ppb increase in carbon monoxide and ozone, the school absenteeism rate would increase 3.79% and 13.01%, respectively. PM_{10} was negatively correlated with absenteeism.
Currie et al., 2007	1996–2001, Texas	Carbon monoxide	School absences	Difference-in-differences strategy controlling for characteristics of schools, years, and attendance periods	Authors reported a significant effect of carbon monoxide on school absences, when carbon monoxide exceeded air quality standards and when carbon monoxide was 75–100% of standards.
Gilliland et al., 2001	1996, California	Ozone, NO_2, PM_{10}	School absenteeism	Two-stage time-series model; considered potential sources of bias, such as incomplete control of temporal trends and temperature effects, as well as incomplete ascertainment through sensitivity analyses	Short-term change in ozone was associated with increase in school absences due to upper- and lower-respiratory illnesses. An increase of 20 ppb ozone was associated with increases of 63% for illness-related absence rates, 83% for respiratory illnesses, 45% for upper-respiratory illnesses, and 174% for LRIs with wet cough.

Table A.2—Continued

Author and Year Published	Study Date and Location	Key Pollutant or Regulation	Key Outcome	Main Methods, Assumptions, and Types of Evidence	Main Findings
Mohai et al., 2011	2006–2007, Michigan	Emission data from EPA TRI	Academic performance and student attendance	Ecological study design correlating air pollution levels around public schools with outcomes, controlling for school location, spending per student, and school-level socioeconomic variables	Schools located in areas with the highest air pollution levels tended to have the lowest attendance rates and the largest proportion of students failing state educational testing standards.
Peters et al., 1997	1991–1992, Sokolov, Czech Republic	TSPs, PM_{10}, SO_2, particle strong acidity (PSA), sulfates (SO_4)	School absences	Logistic regression models, which included a linear trend, temperature, and indicators of day of the week	SO_2 and PSA were significantly associated with school absences
Ransom and Pope, 1992	1985–1990, Utah	PM_{10}	School absenteeism	Absenteeism was regressed on PM_{10} levels, temperature, snowfall, and time variables.	PM_{10} was significantly associated with absenteeism. An increase in 28-day moving average PM_{10} of 100 μg/m^3 was associated with an increase in overall absences equal to about 40%.

Table A.2—Continued

Author and Year Published	Study Date and Location	Key Pollutant or Regulation	Key Outcome	Main Methods, Assumptions, and Types of Evidence	Main Findings
Romieu et al., 1992	1991, Mexico City	PM_{10}, $PM_{2.5}$, ozone	Exacerbation of childhood asthma	Generalized estimating equations models assessing relationships between increases in pollution and peak expiratory flow rate and daily respiratory symptoms, such as lower-respiratory illness (LRI)	An increase of 20 μg/m^3 of PM_{10} was associated with an 8% increase in LRI on the same day. An increase of 10 μg/m^3 in weekly mean $PM_{2.5}$ was related to a 21% increase in LRI. An increase of 50 ppb in ozone was associated with a 9% increase in LRI.
Zweig, Ham, and Avol, 2009	1998–2002; 2004–2005, California	PM_{10}, $PM_{2.5}$, NO_2, ozone	Academic performance (math and reading scores)	Regression models with school fixed effects and controlling for potential confounders	Study indicated that a 10% decrease in PM_{10}, $PM_{2.5}$, or NO_2 would raise math test scores by 0.15%, 0.34%, or 0.18%. A 10% decrease in $PM_{2.5}$ would increase reading scores by 0.21%.

Table A.3
Literature on Air Quality and Quality of Life

Author and Year Published	Study Date and Location	Key Pollutant or Regulation	Key Outcome	Main Methods, Assumptions, and Types of Evidence	Main Findings
Chapko and Solomon, 1976	1972–1973, New York City	SO_2, smokeshade, carbon monoxide, oxidants	Attendance at recreational sites	Regressions of attendance on pollution measures	Higher oxidant concentrations are associated with lower attendance at one recreational site. Higher carbon monoxide concentrations are associated with lower attendance at one site but higher attendance at another.
Di Tella and MacCulloch, 2008	1975–1997, 12 Organisation for Economic Co-operation and Development countries	SO_x	Life satisfaction	Panel regression of life satisfaction measures on SO_x, controlling for country and time fixed effects, as well as country-level variables	Lower levels of SO_x are associated with higher life satisfaction measures.
Gabriel, Mattey, and Wascher, 2003	1981–1990, United States	Ozone, carbon monoxide, environmental regulation, number of hazardous-waste sites	Implicit "price" associated with amenities (including cleaner air)	Estimation of a system of three equations for wages, quality-adjusted housing costs, and cost of living as a function of locational amenities, including ozone and carbon monoxide	The number of hazardous-waste sites and lower air quality are associated with negative implicit prices.
Levinson, 2009	1984–1996, United States	PM_{10}, ozone, SO_2, carbon monoxide	Self-reported happiness	Regression of self-reported happiness measures on pollution levels. Controls for county and year fixed effects	Higher levels of PM_{10} are associated with lower levels of happiness. Results are negative but not statistically significant for other pollutants.

Table A.3—Continued

Author and Year Published	Study Date and Location	Key Pollutant or Regulation	Key Outcome	Main Methods, Assumptions, and Types of Evidence	Main Findings
Luechinger, 2009	1985–2003, Germany	SO_2	Life satisfaction	Longitudinal regression of life satisfaction measures on SO_2, which is instrumented by a regulation requiring scrubbers at power plants. Controls for individual fixed effects, time trends, and other characteristics	Lower levels of SO_2 are associated with higher life satisfaction measures.
Luechinger, 2010	1979–1994, European Union and Norway	SO_2	Life satisfaction	Regression of life satisfaction on SO_2 concentrations. Controls for personal, household characteristics, and economic variables	Lower levels of SO_2 are associated with higher life satisfaction measures.
Neidell, 2006	1989–1997, California	Smog alerts for ozone	Attendance at three outdoor facilities	Regressions of attendance on forecasted ozone (which determines smog alerts), using a regression discontinuity design to compare days with forecasted ozone just above or below the threshold for issuing an alert	Attendance at three outdoor facilities declines by 2–11% when smog alerts are announced, but the effect declines when alerts become more frequent.
Welsch, 2006	1990–1997, Several European countries	NO_2, TSP, lead	Life satisfaction	Longitudinal regression of life satisfaction on pollution measures. Controls for country and time fixed effects	Lower NO_2 and lead concentrations are associated with higher life satisfaction measures.

Table A.4
Literature on Environmental Quality and Individual Location Decisions

Author and Year Published	Study Date and Location	Key Pollutant or Regulation	Key Outcome	Main Methods, Assumptions, and Types of Evidence	Main Findings
Banzhaf and Walsh, 2008	1990–2000, California	Toxicity-weighted index of TRI emissions	Demographic counts	Regression of change in population from 1990 to 2000 as a function of lagged exposure to TRI emissions. Controls for local-area fixed effects and other characteristics	Increased exposure to TRI emissions is associated with decreases in demographic counts.
Bayer, Keohane, and Timmins, 2009	1990–2000, United States	PM	Housing values	Two-stage model, in which first stage involves a discrete-choice model to estimate the utility of living in a metro area (to account for the fact that moving is costly) and the second stage regresses utility on air pollution concentrations. Air pollution is instrumented with pollution from distant sources.	Estimated elasticity of WTP with respect to air quality of 0.34–0.42, implying that the median household would be willing to pay \$149–\$185 in 1982–1984 dollars for a 1-μg/m^3 reduction in PM.

Table A.4—Continued

Author and Year Published	Study Date and Location	Key Pollutant or Regulation	Key Outcome	Main Methods, Assumptions, and Types of Evidence	Main Findings
Cebula and Alexander, 2006	2000–2004, United States	Hazardous-waste sites, toxic-chemical releases	Net in-migration rate	Regression of net in-migration rate to a state between 2000 and 2004 on percentage distribution of hazardous-waste sites in the state on the National Priorities List and per capita toxic-chemical releases in the state. Controls for various state characteristics and economic conditions	Higher prevalence of hazardous-waste sites and chemical releases are associated with lower net in-migration rates.
Chay and Greenstone, 2005	1970–1980, United States	TSP	Housing values	Hedonic regression of housing values on mean TSP by county. Uses nonattainment status as an instrument for TSP change, comparing counties just above or below the threshold for nonattainment. Controls for observable county characteristics and region fixed effects	Elasticity of housing values with respect to TSP ranges from –0.20 to –0.35.

Table A.4—Continued

Author and Year Published	Study Date and Location	Key Pollutant or Regulation	Key Outcome	Main Methods, Assumptions, and Types of Evidence	Main Findings
Foster, 1977	1974–1976, United States and Canada	"Clean environment"	Importance of various quality-of-life factors	Survey of 8,846 firms in the United States and Canada that asked respondents about trade-offs between economic factors and quality-of-life issues	Among U.S. respondents, "clean environment" was ranked as "important personally" by 56% of respondents; "important to plant operation" by 30% of respondents, and "important to key personnel" by 40% of respondents.
Gottlieb, 1994	1962–1992, various	Environmental quality	Amenity rankings	Review of eight studies that surveyed firms about amenities	Average rank for "environmental quality" is third among all firms, first among high-tech firms.
Hekman, 1982	1978–1982, North Carolina, South Carolina, and Virginia	Quality of air and water	Rankings of quality-of-life factors	Survey of business executives on the importance of various economic and quality-of-life factors	Air and water quality were among the top-ranked quality-of-life factors. Quality-of-life factors were typically considered less important than economic factors.

Table A.4—Continued

Author and Year Published	Study Date and Location	Key Pollutant or Regulation	Key Outcome	Main Methods, Assumptions, and Types of Evidence	Main Findings
Malecki and Bradbury, 1992	1988, United States	Environmental quality	Ratings of attributes considered important in locational choices	Surveys of research and development facilities and professional and technical workers at those facilities.	Firms ranked environmental quality as fifth in terms of needs at their present sites and first in terms of needs at their "ideal" sites, as well as needs for their employees. Workers ranked environmental quality as fifth at their present sites and second at their "ideal" sites.
Porell, 1982	1965–1970, United States, 25 MSAs	TSP, SO_2, annual inversion frequency (factor score from first principal component index)	Migration between metropolitan areas	Three-stage "gravity" model of migration as a function of population, economic, and quality-of-life variables. Controls for metro-area fixed effects	Air pollution variable is negatively correlated with in-migration. Implied elasticities of in-migration are –0.039, –0.041, and –0.019 for TSP, SO_2, and annual inversion frequency, respectively.
Smith and Huang, 1995	1967–1988, various	PM	Housing values	Meta-analysis of 37 studies estimating the relationship between PM concentrations and housing values	Estimated marginal WTP for a 1-$\mu g/m^3$ reduction in TSP has a mean of $109.90 and a median of $22.40, with an interquartile range from $0 to $98.52 in 1982–1984 dollars.

Table A.5
Literature on Air Quality Regulations and Firm Location Decisions

Author and Year Published	Study Date and Location	Key Pollutant or Regulation	Key Outcome	Main Methods, Assumptions, and Types of Evidence	Main Findings
Greenstone, List, and Syverson, 2012	1972–1993, United States	Nonattainment status for ozone	Plant exits, total factor productivity (TFP)	Plant-level panel regression of TFP and plant exit on interaction between county's nonattainment status and being in a pollution-intensive industry. Controls for plant-level fixed effects	Among surviving plants in polluting industries, nonattainment status is associated with lower TFP and greater likelihood of plant exit.
Jeppesen, List, and Folmer, 2002	1963–1990, various	Environmental regulation measures (various)	Various measures of firm location, new firm births, and foreign direct investment	Methods of included studies vary but are typically based on regression methods.	First wave of studies typically did not find robust association between regulations and firm location. Second wave tended to find that regulations have a negative effect on firm location.
List, McHone, and Millimet, 2003	1980–1990, New York State	Nonattainment status for ozone	Number of new relocating plants in pollution-intensive industries	Two methods are used to examine relationship between nonattainment status and relocation choices; (1) count model with county fixed effects and (2) propensity score matching of attainment and nonattainment areas.	Nonattainment status is associated with fewer new relocating plants in pollution-intensive industries, although the results are not always statistically significant.

Table A.5—Continued

Author and Year Published	Study Date and Location	Key Pollutant or Regulation	Key Outcome	Main Methods, Assumptions, and Types of Evidence	Main Findings
List, Millimet, Fredriksson, et al., 2003	1980–1990, New York State	Nonattainment status for ozone	Number of new plants in pollution-intensive industries	Propensity score estimator used to match nonattainment and attainment areas to examine the relationship between nonattainment and new plant formations	Nonattainment status is generally associated with fewer new plants in pollution-intensive industries, although results are not always statistically significant.
List, Millimet, and McHone, 2004	1980–1990, New York State	Nonattainment status for ozone	Plant modifications and closures	Two methods are used to examine relationship between nonattainment status and plant modifications or closures: (1) count model with county fixed effects and (2) propensity score matching of attainment and nonattainment areas.	Nonattainment status is generally associated with fewer plant modifications, but there is no systematic relationship between nonattainment status and plant closures.
Morgan and Condliffe, 2009	1996–2000, United States	Nonattainment status for ozone, particulates, carbon monoxide, and SO_2	New births of polluting plants	Count model with fixed effects of plant births on nonattainment status. Includes county fixed effects and other controls	Nonattainment status for ozone and PM is negatively associated with plant births in pollution-intensive industries.

Table A.6
Literature on Air Quality Regulations and Cost and Productivity

Author and Year Published	Study Date and Location	Key Pollutant or Regulation	Key Outcome	Main Methods, Assumptions, and Types of Evidence	Main Findings
Becker, 2005	1979–1988, United States	Nonattainment status	Air pollution abatement expenditures	Regression of firm air pollution abatement expenditures on nonattainment status interacted with whether a firm is a high emitter of a regulated pollutant. Controls for county-by-year fixed effects and firm characteristics	Pollution-intensive firms in nonattainment areas generally had higher air pollution abatement expenditures, although the magnitude and statistical significance of the results varies by pollutant and regression method.
Berman and Bui, 2001	1979–1992, South Coast Air Quality Management District	Local air pollution regulations for oil refineries	Productivity of oil refineries	Comparison of TFP changes from 1982 to 1992 in South Coast Air Quality Management District, which faced more-stringent regulations, and the rest of the United States	South Coast refineries experienced an increase in productivity, relative to U.S. refineries, during a time when pollution regulations were increased to a greater extent in South Coast.

Table A.6—Continued

Author and Year Published	Study Date and Location	Key Pollutant or Regulation	Key Outcome	Main Methods, Assumptions, and Types of Evidence	Main Findings
Boyd and McClelland, 1999	1988–1992, United States	SO_2 and TSP emissions (to air); biological oxygen demand and total suspended solids (to water); and chlorine, methane, and sulfuric acid (toxic)	Efficiency among integrated paper mills	Examines the relationship between plant efficiency and pollutant emissions to examine whether there are cases in which plants could reduce input usage and pollution emission (while maintaining productivity). Models pollution regulations by removing the assumption of free disposal for pollution, and measures output loss due to pollution regulations using the distance of the plant from the production set boundary	Production is 9% lower due to environmental constraints. However, the paper industry may be able to reduce both inputs and pollution by 2–8% while maintaining the same level of productivity.
EPA, 2011a	1990–2020 (projections), United States	VOC, NO_x, carbon monoxide, SO_2, PM_{10}, $PM_{2.5}$, ammonia	Direct cost estimates of compliance with the 1990 Clean Air Act Amendments	Estimated direct costs using a combination of per-unit cost measures and least-cost optimization measures	Direct cost of compliance with 1990 amendments is estimated to be \$19.9 billion in 2000, \$53 billion in 2010, and \$65.5 billion in 2020 (in 2006 dollars).

Table A.6—Continued

Author and Year Published	Study Date and Location	Key Pollutant or Regulation	Key Outcome	Main Methods, Assumptions, and Types of Evidence	Main Findings
Gray and Shadbegian, 1995	1979–1990, United States	Pollution expenditure, compliance status, enforcement activity, and emissions	TFP in paper, oil, and steel industries	Cross-sectional and panel regressions of TFP on various measures of pollution regulation	Cross-sectional regression results indicate that higher abatement costs are correlated with lower productivity. Panel regression results do not indicate a statistically significant relationship between abatement costs and productivity. No statistically significant relationship was found between other measures of regulations and productivity.
Hammitt, 2000	1986–1988, United States	Chlorofluorocarbons (CFCs)	Costs of compliance with the Montreal Protocol on Substances That Deplete the Ozone Layer (Ozone Secretariat, 1988)	Compares cost estimates from ex ante and ex post studies of implementation of the Montreal Protocol	Ex ante estimates substantially overestimate the cost of limiting trichlorofluoromethane and difluorodichloromethane consumption and modestly underestimate cost of limiting trichlorotrifluoroethane consumption. Ex post estimates underestimate the marginal cost of limiting CFC consumption.

Table A.6—Continued

Author and Year Published	Study Date and Location	Key Pollutant or Regulation	Key Outcome	Main Methods, Assumptions, and Types of Evidence	Main Findings
Harrington, Morgenstern, and Nelson, 2000	Largely United States, some international	Various	Costs of compliance with 28 rules (including multiple environmental regulations)	Compares ex ante estimates of the direct cost of compliance with 28 regulations with ex post estimates	Ex ante estimates overestimated costs in 14 cases and underestimated costs in three cases (out of 28). For EPA regulations, ex ante estimates overestimated cost in seven cases and underestimated cost in two cases (out of 13).
Jaffe and Palmer, 1997	1974–1991, United States	Environmental compliance expenditures	Research and development expenditures and patent counts	Panel regression of R&D expenditures and patent counts on pollution abatement expenditures by industry. Controls for industry characteristics and industry and time fixed effects	Lagged environmental compliance expenditures are associated with higher R&D expenditures but not with patent counts.
Jaffe, Peterson, et al., 1995	1970–1980 (for productivity outcomes), various	Environmental regulations	Firm productivity (and other outcomes)	Survey of existing literature on environmental regulations and U.S. manufacturing firms	With respect to productivity, environmental regulations accounted for 8–16% of the productivity slowdown of the 1970s.
Lanjouw and Mody, 1996	1971–1988, United States, Germany, and Japan	Pollution abatement expenditures	Share of patents in pollution control technology	Descriptive analysis of relationships between pollution abatement expenditures and patent shares	Pollution abatement expenditures appear to be related to subsequent patenting in related fields.

Table A.6—Continued

Author and Year Published	Study Date and Location	Key Pollutant or Regulation	Key Outcome	Main Methods, Assumptions, and Types of Evidence	Main Findings
Lanoie, Patry, and Lajeunesse, 2008	1985–1994, Quebec	Ratio of the value of pollution control equipment to total cost in an industry during a time period	Industry productivity for 17 sectors	Panel regression of TFP on environmental regulation at the industry level. Controls for industrial characteristics and industry and time fixed effects	Contemporary environmental regulation is negatively associated with productivity; lagged environmental regulation is positively associated with productivity.
Nelson, Tietenberg, and Donihue, 1993	1969–1983, United States	Value of electric utility's air (and total) pollution control equipment	Emissions, age of capital	Three-stage regressions relating age of capital, emissions, and regulations faced by 44 electric utilities (proxied by value of pollution control equipment)	Higher pollution-related expenditures are associated with increased age of capital among electric utilities and with decreased emissions, but increased age is not associated with emissions.
Popp, 2006	1967–2000, United States, Germany, and Japan	Regulations for NO_x and SO_2	Patent counts	Descriptive analysis of patent counts related to NO_x and SO_2 control techniques following regulations	Patent counts appear to increase in the United States and Germany after regulations were enacted in the country but not after regulations were enacted in other countries.

Table A.7
Literature on Air Quality Regulations and Employment

Author and Year Published	Study Date and Location	Key Pollutant or Regulation	Key Outcome	Main Methods, Assumptions, and Types of Evidence	Main Findings
Duffy-Deno, 1992	1974–1982, United States	Air pollution abatement expenditures in an MSA	Manufacturing earnings and employment in an MSA	Panel regression of manufacturing earnings and employment on air pollution abatement expenditures. Controls for MSA characteristics and fixed effects	Higher pollution abatement expenditures are associated with lower earnings and employment, although the relationship is not always statistically significant.
Greenstone, 2002	1967–1987, United States	Nonattainment status for carbon monoxide, ozone, SO_2, and TSP	Employment, capital stock, and shipments	Plant-level panel regression of percentage change in manufacturing activity on interaction between county's nonattainment status and being in a pollution-intensive industry. Controls for plant-level fixed effects and county and industry trends	Nonattainment status is associated with lower employment, although the results vary to some extent across regulated pollutants.
Morgenstern, Pizer, and Shih, 2002	1979–1991, United States	Pollution abatement expenditures	Employment in four industries. Focus on effect of regulations on employment via three channels: cost effect, factor-shift effect, and demand effect	Estimate a structural cost model and demand elasticities, which are, in turn, used to estimate effects on each of the three channels	Across the four industries, increased pollution abatement expenditures are associated with a net gain of 1.5 jobs per $1 million in incremental expenditure, but the relationship is not statistically significant.

Table A.7—Continued

Author and Year Published	Study Date and Location	Key Pollutant or Regulation	Key Outcome	Main Methods, Assumptions, and Types of Evidence	Main Findings
Walker, 2012	1990–2000, United States	1990 Clean Air Act Amendments	Employment and earnings	Panel regression of earnings on county's nonattainment status and being employed in a pollution-intensive industry. Examines the effect of regulations on polluting sectors in newly designated nonattainment areas, while controlling for trends in county outcomes and in sectoral outcomes	Following the 1990 amendments, workers in newly regulated plants experienced wage losses for approximately eight years.

APPENDIX B

Interview Protocol

This appendix presents the interview protocol we used for the study.

Introduction

We are conducting a study on the links between air quality and economic development in Allegheny County. The project is part of the Breathe Initiative Project sponsored by the Heinz Endowments.

Southwestern Pennsylvania has made enormous progress in reducing air pollution over the last few decades but still does not achieve the EPA's standards for two air pollutants (ozone and particulate matter) and is considered a nonattainment area for these two pollutants. Our goal in this project is to understand the extent to which local air quality, including the region's nonattainment status, may affect local economic development.

We are speaking with firms, community organizations, government agencies, and other local stakeholders to understand how Allegheny County's air quality, or its nonattainment status, might affect the decisions that firms and individuals make, for example, with respect to plant location, day-to-day operations, long-term planning, or housing and recreation choices. These discussions will inform our final report, but any comments made during the interviews will not be attributed to a specific individual or organization.

Introductory Questions

- Do you see Allegheny's air quality as an important concern for the area? If so, in what specific ways does air quality pose a concern?
- Has your organization been involved with any efforts to reduce or manage air pollution in Allegheny County?
- Are you aware of any ways in which air quality has played a role, either positive or negative, in local economic development?

Firm Location Issues

One concern that often comes up when air quality and air quality regulations are discussed is the idea that these factors may affect the decisions of firms to locate here.

- Before choosing to open or relocate to this area, did you consider other locations? Which other locations did you consider, and why did you choose your current location?
- To what extent, if at all, did Allegheny County's air quality, or environmental regulations targeted at improving air quality, affect your firm's decision to locate here?
- If air quality played a role in your location decision, was it air quality directly that mattered or was it the regulatory measures that are in place to improve air quality? In what way did these issues affect your location decision?
- Do Allegheny County's air quality or environmental regulations targeted at improving air quality affect your planning in terms of expansion or future site location?
- Did Allegheny County's environmental regulations targeted at improving air quality affect your decision to locate here?
- What are the key factors that firms consider when deciding whether to open or expand operations in Allegheny County?
- To what extent, if at all, do Allegheny County's air quality or environmental regulations targeted at improving air quality affect firms' decisions to locate or expand here?
- Are there specific types of firms that are more affected by local air quality or environmental regulations targeted at improving local air quality?
- If air quality plays a role in firm location decisions, is it air quality directly that matters or [are effects on those decisions] because of regulatory measures that are in place to improve air quality? In what way do these issues affect firm location decisions?
- Can you think of any firms that considered locating in Allegheny County but did not come here? What were the major factors in that decision? Did air quality directly, or environmental regulations to achieve better air quality, play any role?

Day-to-Day Operations and Employment

We would also like to discuss the extent to which air quality may affect firms' day-to-day operations or decisions.

- Do Allegheny County's air quality or environmental regulations targeted at improving air quality affect your firm's operating costs?

- Do Allegheny County's air quality or environmental regulations targeted at improving air quality affect the number or types of workers you hire?
- Do Allegheny County's air quality or environmental regulations targeted at improving air quality affect your decisions about when or how to upgrade your equipment?
- Do Allegheny County's air quality or environmental regulations targeted at improving air quality affect [your] major investors (or potential investors') decisions about whether and how much to invest locally?
- Does Allegheny County's air quality affect your workers' performance or absences in any way? If so, are there specific types of workers who are affected?
- Are you aware of any ways in which Allegheny County's air quality affects [your] firm's health care costs?
- Are there any other ways in which Allegheny County's air quality or environmental regulations targeted at improving air quality affect your day-to-day operations?

Worker Location and Other Household Issues

We are also interested in your opinion about whether residents consider air quality issues when deciding whether to move into or out of Allegheny County, or where to live.

- From where does your firm [or do local firms] typically recruit workers?
- Are most of your members originally from the local area? If not, where do they typically come from?
- Do you ever have trouble hiring workers? If so, are there specific types of workers whom you tend to have trouble hiring?
- When people are deciding whether to live in Allegheny County, what other areas do they usually consider?
- What are the major factors people consider when deciding whether to live in Allegheny County?
- Do potential new residents ever mention barriers to moving to Allegheny County, or key factors in their decisions about whether to relocate? What are the major factors?
- Do current residents who choose to leave the area ever mention reasons for leaving Allegheny County, or key factors in their decisions about whether to relocate? What are the major factors?
- Do potential new residents or residents who choose to leave Allegheny County ever discuss air quality in Allegheny County when making a location decision? If so, are there specific types of workers who are most concerned about air quality issues?

- Do new residents ever ask about air quality when making a decision about where, within the local region, to rent [or] buy a home? If so, are there specific types of residents who are most concerned about air quality issues?
- Do new residents with children ever express concerns about the effect of air quality on child health, school absences, or other issues?
- What are the major factors that students consider when deciding whether to attend [a Pittsburgh-area university]? Does air quality play any role?

Tourism and Broader Regional Issues

We would like to discuss whether air quality issues play any role in local tourism and other, related issues in the area.

- What are the major issues that local residents consider when deciding where to spend their vacations?
- Do local residents often take day trips to local recreational areas?
- What types of activities do local residents typically do on local day trips?
- Does Allegheny County's air quality affect local residents' decisions about whether to take local day trips, or what activities to do?
- What are the major issues that nonresidents consider when deciding whether to take a vacation in Allegheny County?
- What types of activities do nonresidents do on vacation in Allegheny County?
- Does air quality play any role in nonresidents' decisions about whether to take vacations in Allegheny County, or what activities to do?
- Are you aware of any ways in which air quality affects the region's agriculture?
- Are you aware of any ways in which air quality affects the region's ecosystems?

Planning Issues

Finally, we would like to discuss what role, if any, air quality plays in long-term, regional planning issues.

- To what extent is Allegheny County's air quality a consideration in planning decisions with respect to transportation, commercial and residential development, or other issues?
- If air quality is a consideration in long-term planning, is it air quality directly that matters or is [any effect] because of regulatory measures that are in place to improve air quality?
- What are the major challenges to achieving national air quality standards in Allegheny County?

Wrap-Up

We will be using the information gathered during our interviews, along with a review of the literature on air quality and economic development, to inform our final report. As we mentioned at the beginning, any comments made during the interviews will not be attributed to a specific individual or organization. The final report will be available to the public and should be ready by the end of the year.

- Are there any other ways that we have not discussed in which you feel that air quality affects local economic development?
- What would change for your organization if air quality were considerably better or were better than most cities of Pittsburgh's size? What would change for the region?
- What other people or organizations would you suggest we speak to about air quality and economic development issues in Allegheny County?

APPENDIX C

Site Selection Process

This appendix summarizes our discussions with site selection firms regarding the process they use to help firms select new sites.

Overview of the Site Selection Process

The firms we interviewed indicated that they often begin by conducting an initial screening. This screening may be nationwide, or it may be limited to a geographic region requested by the client. The screening criteria are specific to the individual client but often include ease of access to suppliers, customers, and resources and the availability and cost of qualified labor.

Interviewees indicated that certain screening criteria might be relevant to only some firms. For example, firms siting a headquarters may consider direct connections for airline flights a critical component of access to suppliers and customers. Businesses that will emit significant amounts of pollution from a new plant will consider whether an area is in attainment with the NAAQS. Those that are concerned about recruiting employees to a new location will consider quality-of-life factors, such as housing prices, school quality, access to public transit, crime, and the culture and amenities of a potential site. This may be particularly true for clients that expect to recruit employees from outside the region, such as a headquarters or a high-technology firm.

Once a short list of several regions has been developed, other factors also become important. Again, these factors depend on the specific client but often include availability of developed sites; access to infrastructure; governance and regulatory issues, such as taxes, incentives, or ease of permitting; utility costs; and (for clients expecting to recruit employees from outside the region) quality of life for employees. These factors can vary within a region and can play an important role in the selection of the final, specific site.

Air Quality and the Site Selection Process

Our interviews with site selection firms and businesses generally suggested that air quality specifically was not usually an important factor considered by firms when thinking about attracting employees to a region. Nonetheless, we did hear some anecdotal evidence that certain sensitive populations do respond to days with poor air quality by avoiding the outdoors and that some potential recruits do conduct research on air quality in the Pittsburgh region prior to deciding whether to relocate there. One site selection firm representative indicated that air quality issues did come up in terms of worker recruiting, generally for relocations involving national recruiting or a large number of transferees.

Two site selection firms also indicated that certain types of firms—for example, high-technology companies or "green" industry firms—might decide not to locate in nonattainment areas, particularly those that are considered "severe" nonattainment areas or those that are not working to address their air quality issues. The decision would be for strategic reasons (for example, because of reputational issues for the company), as well as concerns among employees and other stakeholders, even those not moving to the area.

Air Quality Regulations in Nonattainment Areas

Several site selection firms indicated that permitting takes significantly longer in nonattainment areas than in attainment areas; one interviewee noted that, in some cases, the process could take up to two or three years. The main reason for the longer time frame is that the new source would be required to show that it meets the LAER requirements and to conduct modeling necessary to show that it would not have a significant impact on air quality. These activities, coupled with review of the modeling by local regulators and public comment, would increase the permitting time.

Offsets would also be required for major sources locating in nonattainment areas. Our discussions with local regulators indicate that this issue is a potential challenge in Pittsburgh. In Pennsylvania, firms that shut down or that reduce their emissions below required standards can "bank" offsets with the Pennsylvania Department of Environmental Protection (DEP). A firm seeking to expand or move into the area can either reduce its own existing emissions (in the case of an expansion) or purchase offsets from another firm; DEP serves as a broker in such an exchange. Our interviews indicated that offsets for ozone precursors (NO_x and VOCs) are generally available in the region but that offsets for $PM_{2.5}$ have not been available for several years. Therefore, a new firm that would be a major $PM_{2.5}$ emitter would find it difficult to locate in the state.

Several site selection firms indicated that facilities that would be considered major emission sources typically avoid nonattainment areas altogether. For a facility that is not expected to be a major source of emissions, our interviews suggested that nonattainment status does not play a role in the siting decision.

Some interviewees suggested that, for major emitters, the elimination of nonattainment areas would take place during a preliminary screening of locations. In other cases, environmental regulations might play a role after a short list of areas has been selected, at which point an environmental engineering firm would often be engaged. One site selection firm indicated that it interviews other firms in the local area to determine how long it would take to get permits, including air and water permits. A projected timeline of more than three to four months would be considered a disadvantage for the area. In general, representatives of site selection firms and major emitters indicated that the concern about nonattainment areas centered not on additional costs but rather on the increased length of time and uncertainty surrounding permitting and offset issues.[1]

Our discussions with site selection firms indicated that the screening process is affected by many factors, particularly after the short list has been determined. For example, during the initial screening, only current attainment status might be used. However, attainment history might be taken into account in later stages, and a major emission source may exclude an area just below the nonattainment threshold. In addition, some major emitters might have a compelling reason to locate in a nonattainment area, which could outweigh the costs and uncertainties associated with nonattainment status. We were also told that screening based on nonattainment might not end up playing a major role in selection. For example, one representative noted that an entire metropolitan area might be screened out if one county is out of attainment; however, such areas may already have been screened out based on labor costs.

---

[1] Our interviews with Allegheny County regulators indicated that the permitting process for a major emission source attempting to expand or locate there would take about 12 months, versus four to six months for a nonmajor source.

APPENDIX D

Detailed Health Benefit Estimates

This appendix presents estimates of the health benefits associated with reducing $PM_{2.5}$ concentrations from 2012 levels to the current NAAQS. Table D.1 presents the results for all key health endpoints covered in Table 4.1 in Chapter Four, while Table D.2 presents the more-detailed results for WLDs. In both cases, the estimated effects on incidence and the associated valuations are presented for meeting the yearly and daily scenarios separately. We present the results separately here in order to present the associated uncertainty (expressed as standard deviations). When combined, the numbers from the two scenarios add up to the values presented in Tables 4.1 and 4.3 in Chapter Four.

Table D.1
Effect That Meeting the New $PM_{2.5}$ Standard Could Have on Key Health Endpoints: Yearly and Daily Scenarios

		Incidence		Valuation ($ thousands)	
Endpoint	Standard Scenario	Mean	Standard Deviation	Amount	Standard Deviation
Acute bronchitis	Yearly	40	23	15	9
	Daily	32	19	12	7
Acute myocardial infarction	Yearly	5	2	246	110
	Daily	4	2	200	90
Asthma exacerbation	Yearly	845	423	132	67
	Daily	681	341	106	54
Chronic bronchitis	Yearly	23	11	3,539	1,642
	Daily	19	9	2,866	1,330
Emergency-room visits, respiratory	Yearly	21	11	6	3
	Daily	17	9	4	2
Hospital admissions, cardiovascular	Yearly	9	4	228	109
	Daily	7	4	186	89
Hospital admissions, respiratory	Yearly	10	2	221	45
	Daily	8	2	181	37
Premature adult mortality	Yearly	49	11	268,339	128,482
	Daily	40	9	217,846	104,312
Upper-respiratory symptoms	Yearly	733	286	19	11
	Daily	590	231	15	9
WLDs	Yearly	4,003	293	474	35
	Daily	3,240	237	384	28
Total Yearly				267,267	121,288
Total daily				220,526	98,105
Total				487,793	

SOURCE: Authors' calculations using EPA's BenMAP software, with ambient air quality values updated to reflect 2012 concentrations in the Pittsburgh MSA.

NOTE: The total valuation is based on a Monte Carlo simulation of the underlying results for each endpoint and is therefore not equal to the sum of the individual valuations.

Table D.2
Detailed Results for the Effect That Meeting the $PM_{2.5}$ Standard Could Have on Work-Loss Days: Yearly and Daily Scenarios

		WLDs		Valuation ($)	
Incidence	Standard Scenario	Number Avoided	Standard Deviation	Amount	Standard Deviation
Large MSA	Yearly	7,281	533	958,190	70,183
	Daily	5,893	432	775,539	56,817
Midwest	Yearly	7,294	534	959,912	70,309
	Daily	5,904	433	776,933	56,920
Northeast	Yearly	8,178	599	1,076,195	78,827
	Daily	6,619	485	871,051	63,815

SOURCE: Authors' calculations using EPA's BenMAP software, with ambient air quality values updated to reflect 2012 concentrations in the Pittsburgh MSA.

NOTE: We assumed that the Pittsburgh MSA would meet the annual standard first and then employ strategies to meet the daily standard.

APPENDIX E

Industry Codes

Tables E.1 and E.2 show the mapping we used to translate SIC codes into NAICS codes for pollution-intensive industries.

Table E.1
Industries Included in Establishment Estimates

Industry	SIC Code	NAICS Code
Industrial organic chemicals	286	32511, 325132, and 32519
Petroleum refining	291	324110
Plastic materials and synthetics	282	3252
Miscellaneous plastics	308	3261
Primary steel	331	331111 and 3312

Table E.2
Industries Included in Output and Employment Estimates

Industry	SIC Code	NAICS Code
Printing	2711–2789	323
Organic chemicals	286	32511, 325132, and 32519
Rubber and miscellaneous plastic products	30	326
Fabricated metals	34	332
Motor vehicles, bodies, and parts	371	3361, 3362, and 3363
Lumber and wood products	24	113310 and 321
Petroleum refining	291	324110
Stone, clay, glass, and concrete	32	327
Pulp and paper	2611–2631	3221
Iron and steel	3312–3313 and 3321–3325	3311, 3312, and 33151

References

Abt Associates, *BenMAP Environmental Benefits Mapping and Analysis Program: User's Manual Appendices*, Research Triangle Park, N.C.: U.S. Environmental Protection Agency, Office of Air Quality Planning and Standards, October 2012. As of November 5, 2013:
http://www.epa.gov/airquality/benmap/models/BenMAPAppendicesOct2012.pdf

Banzhaf, H. Spencer, and Randall P. Walsh, "Do People Vote with Their Feet? An Empirical Test of Tiebout's Mechanism," *American Economic Review*, Vol. 98, No. 3, June 2008, pp. 843–863.

Bayer, Patrick, Nathaniel Keohane, and Christopher Timmins, "Migration and Hedonic Valuation: The Case of Air Quality," *Journal of Environmental Economics and Management*, Vol. 58, No. 1, July 2009, pp. 1–14.

Becker, Randy A., "Air Pollution Abatement Costs Under the Clean Air Act: Evidence from the PACE Survey," *Journal of Environmental Economics and Management*, Vol. 50, No. 1, July 2005, pp. 144–169.

Bell, Michelle L., "The Use of Ambient Air Quality Modeling to Estimate Individual and Population Exposure for Human Health Research: A Case Study of Ozone in the Northern Georgia Region of the United States," *Environmental International*, Vol. 32, No. 5, July 2006, pp. 586–593.

Berman, Eli, and Linda T. M. Bui, "Environmental Regulation and Productivity: Evidence from Oil Refineries," *Review of Economics and Statistics*, Vol. 83, No. 3, August 2001, pp. 498–510.

BLS—*See* Bureau of Labor Statistics.

Boyd, Gale A., and John D. McClelland, "The Impact of Environmental Constraints on Productivity Improvement in Integrated Paper Plants," *Journal of Environmental Economics and Management*, Vol. 38, No. 2, September 1999, pp. 121–142.

Broadhurst, Karen E., Corinne A. May-Chahal, and Helen Paton, "Children Missing from School Systems: Exploring Divergent Patterns of Disengagement in the Narrative Accounts of Parents, Carers, Children and Young People," *British Journal of Sociology of Education*, Vol. 26, No. 1, 2005, pp. 105–119.

Brunnermeier, Smita B., and Arik Levinson, "Examining the Evidence on Environmental Regulations and Industry Location," *Journal of Environment and Development*, Vol. 13, No. 6, March 2004, pp. 6–41.

Bureau of Labor Statistics, *May 2011 Occupational Employment and Wage Estimates: Metropolitan Area Cross-Industry Estimates*, c. 2011a. As of August 2, 2013:
http://www.bls.gov/oes/oes_dl.htm

———, *Highlights of Women's Earnings in 2010*, Report 1031, July 22, 2011b. As of November 13, 2013:
http://www.bls.gov/cps/cpswom2010.pdf

Carnegie Mellon University, *Air Toxics in Allegheny County: Sources, Airborne Concentrations, and Human Exposure*, Pittsburgh, Pa.: Allegheny County Health Department, March 2009. As of November 5, 2013:
http://www.achd.net/air/pubs/pdf/CMU%20Air%20Toxics%20FINAL%20REPORT%20REVISED%20MAR%2009.pdf

Carson, Richard T., Yongil Jeon, and Donald R. McCubbin, "The Relationship Between Air Pollution Emissions and Income: U.S. Data," *Environment and Development Economics*, Vol. 2, No. 4, November 1997, pp. 433–450.

Cebula, Richard J., and Gigi M. Alexander, "Determinants of Net Interstate Migration, 2000–2004," *Journal of Regional Analysis and Policy*, Vol. 36, No. 2, 2006, pp. 116–123.

Centers for Disease Control and Prevention, "Summary Health Statistics for U.S. Adults: National Health Interview Survey, 2010," *Vital and Health Statistics*, Series 10, No. 252, January 2012. As of November 5, 2013:
http://www.cdc.gov/nchs/data/series/sr_10/sr10_252.pdf

Chapko, Michael K., and Henry Solomon, "Air Pollution and Recreational Behavior," *Journal of Social Psychology*, Vol. 100, No. 1, 1976, pp. 149–150.

Chay, Kenneth Y., and Michael Greenstone, "Does Air Quality Matter? Evidence from the Housing Market," *Journal of Political Economy*, Vol. 113, No. 2, 2005, pp. 376–424.

Chen, Lei, Brian L. Jennison, Wei Yang, and Stanley T. Omaye, "Elementary School Absenteeism and Air Pollution," *Inhalation Toxicology*, Vol. 12, No. 11, 2000, pp. 997–1016.

CMU—*See* Carnegie Mellon University.

Crocker, Thomas D., and Robert L. Horst Jr., "Hours of Work, Labor Productivity, and Environmental Conditions: A Case Study," *Review of Economics and Statistics*, Vol. 63, No. 3, August 1981, pp. 361–368.

Currie, Janet, Eric Hanushek, E. Megan Kahn, Matthew Neidell, and Steven Rivkin, *Does Pollution Increase School Absences?* Cambridge, Mass.: National Bureau of Economic Research Working Paper 13252, July 2007. As of November 5, 2013:
http://www.nber.org/papers/w13252

Di Tella, Rafael, and Robert MacCulloch, "Gross National Happiness as an Answer to the Easterlin Paradox?" *Journal of Development Economics*, Vol. 86, No. 1, 2008, pp. 22–42.

Duffy-Deno, Kevin T., "Pollution Abatement Expenditures and Regional Manufacturing Activity," *Journal of Regional Science*, Vol. 32, No. 4, November 1992, pp. 419–436.

EPA—*See* U.S. Environmental Protection Agency.

Fisk, W. J., D. Black, and G. Brunner, "Benefits and Costs of Improved IEQ in U.S. Offices," *Indoor Air*, Vol. 21, No. 5, October 2011, pp. 357–367.

Foster, Robert, "Economic and Quality of Life Factors in Industrial Location Decisions," *Social Indicators Research*, Vol. 4, No. 3, July 1977, pp. 247–265.

Gabriel, Stuart A., Joe P. Mattey, and William L. Wascher, "Compensating Differentials and Evolution in the Quality-of-Life Among U.S. States," *Regional Science and Urban Economics*, Vol. 33, No. 5, September 2003, pp. 619–649.

Gilliland, F. D., K. Berhane, E. B. Rappaport, D. C. Thomas, E. Avol, W. J. Gauderman, S. J. London, H. G. Margolis, R. McConnell, K. T. Islam, and J. M. Peters, "The Effects of Ambient Air Pollution on School Absenteeism Due to Respiratory Illnesses," *Epidemiology*, Vol. 12, No. 1, January 2001, pp. 43–54.

Gottfried, Michael A., "Evaluating the Relationship Between Student Attendance and Achievement in Urban Elementary and Middle Schools: An Instrumental Variables Approach," *American Educational Research Journal*, Vol. 47, No. 2, June 2010, pp. 434–465.

Gottlieb, Paul D., "Amenities as an Economic Development Tool: Is There Enough Evidence?" *Economic Development Quarterly*, Vol. 8, No. 3, August 1994, pp. 270–285.

Gough, David, "Weight of Evidence: A Framework for the Appraisal of the Quality and Relevance of Evidence," *Research Papers in Education*, Vol. 22, No. 2, 2007, pp. 213–228.

Graff Zivin, Joshua, and Matthew Neidell, "The Impact of Pollution on Worker Productivity," *American Economic Review*, Vol. 102, No. 7, December 2012, pp. 3652–3673.

Gray, Wayne B., and Ronald J. Shadbegian, *Pollution Abatement Costs, Regulation, and Plant-Level Productivity*, Cambridge, Mass.: National Bureau of Economic Research Working Paper 4994, January 1995. As of November 5, 2013:
http://www.nber.org/papers/w4994

Greenstone, Michael, "The Impacts of Environmental Regulations on Industrial Activity: Evidence from the 1970 and 1977 Clean Air Act Amendments and the Census of Manufactures," *Journal of Political Economy*, Vol. 110, No. 6, December 2002, pp. 1175–1219.

Greenstone, Michael, John A. List, and Chad Syverson, *The Effects of Environmental Regulation on the Competitiveness of U.S. Manufacturing*, Cambridge, Mass.: National Bureau of Economic Research Working Paper 18392, September 2012. As of November 5, 2013:
http://www.nber.org/papers/w18392

Hallfors, Denise, Jack L. Vevea, Bonita Iritani, HyunSan Cho, Shereen Khatapoush, and Leonard Saxe, "Truancy, Grade Point Average, and Sexual Activity: A Meta-Analysis of Risk Indicators for Youth Substance Use," *Journal of School Health*, Vol. 72, No. 5, May 2002, pp. 205–211.

Hammitt, James K., "Are the Costs of Proposed Environmental Regulations Overestimated? Evidence from the CFC Phaseout," *Environmental and Resource Economics*, Vol. 16, 2000, pp. 281–301.

Hanna, Rema, and Paulina Oliva, *The Effect of Pollution on Labor Supply: Evidence from a Natural Experiment in Mexico City*, Cambridge, Mass.: National Bureau of Economic Research Working Paper 17302, August 2011. As of November 5, 2013:
http://www.nber.org/papers/w17302

Hansen, Anett C., and Harald K. Selte, "Air Pollution and Sick-Leaves," *Environmental and Resource Economics*, Vol. 16, 2000, pp. 31–50.

Harrington, Winston, Richard D. Morgenstern, and Peter Nelson, "On the Accuracy of Regulatory Cost Estimates," *Journal of Policy Analysis and Management*, Vol. 19, No. 2, Spring 2000, pp. 297–322.

Hausman, Jerry A., Bart D. Ostro, and David A. Wise, *Air Pollution and Lost Work*, Cambridge, Mass.: National Bureau of Economic Research Working Paper 1263, 1984. As of November 5, 2013:
http://www.nber.org/papers/w1263

Hazilla, Michael, and Raymond J. Kopp, "Social Cost of Environmental Quality Regulations: A General Equilibrium Analysis," *Journal of Political Economy*, Vol. 98, No. 4, August 1990, pp. 853–873.

Hekman, J. S., "Survey of Location Decisions in the South," *Economic Review*, Vol. 6, 1982, pp. 6-19.

Henderson, J. Vernon, "Effects of Air Quality Regulation," *American Economic Review*, Vol. 86, No. 4, September 1996, pp. 789–813.

Hubbell, Bryan J., Aaron Hallberg, Donald R. McCubbin, and Ellen Post, "Health-Related Benefits of Attaining the 8-Hr Ozone Standard," *Environmental Health Perspectives*, Vol. 113, No. 1, January 2005, pp. 73–82.

Jaffe, Adam B., and Karen Palmer, "Environmental Regulation and Innovation: A Panel Data Study," *Review of Economics and Statistics*, Vol. 79, No. 4, November 1997, pp. 610–619.

Jaffe, Adam B., Steven R. Peterson, Paul R. Portney, and Robert N. Stavins, "Environmental Regulation and the Competitiveness of U.S. Manufacturing: What Does the Evidence Tell Us?" *Journal of Economic Literature*, Vol. 33, No. 1, March 1995, pp. 132–163.

Jeppesen, Tim, and Henk Folmer, "The Confusing Relationship Between Environmental Policy and the Location Behaviour of Firms: A Methodological Review of Selected Case Studies," *Annals of Regional Science*, Vol. 35, 2001, pp. 523–546.

Jeppesen, Tim, John A. List, and Henk Folmer, "Environmental Regulations and New Plant Location Decisions: Evidence from a Meta-Analysis," *Journal of Regional Science*, Vol. 42, No. 1, February 2002, pp. 19–49.

Jorgenson, Dale W., and Richard J. Goettle, *An Economic Analysis of the Benefits and Costs of the Clean Air Act, 1970 to 1990: Revised Report and Findings*, Washington, D.C.: National Center for Environmental Economics, U.S. Environmental Protection Agency, August 2001.

Jorgensen, Dale W., and Peter J. Wilcoxen, "Environmental Regulation and U.S. Economic Growth," *RAND Journal of Economics*, Vol. 21, No. 2, Summer 1990, pp. 314–340.

Kane, Jean, "School Exclusions and Masculine, Working-Class Identities," *Gender and Education*, Vol. 18, No. 6, 2006, pp. 673–685.

Lanjouw, Jean Olson, and Ashoka Mody, "Innovation and the International Diffusion of Environmentally Responsive Technology," *Research Policy*, Vol. 25, No. 4, June 1996, pp. 549–571.

Lanoie, Paul, Michel Patry, and Richard Lajeunesse, "Environmental Regulation and Productivity: Testing the Porter Hypothesis," *Journal of Productivity Analysis*, Vol. 30, 2008, pp. 121–128.

Levinson, Arik, *Valuing Public Goods Using Happiness Data: The Case of Air Quality*, Cambridge, Mass.: National Bureau of Economic Research Working Paper 15156, July 2009. As of November 5, 2013:
http://www.nber.org/papers/w15156

List, John A., and W. Warren McHone, "Ranking State Environmental Outputs: Evidence from Panel Data," *Growth and Change*, Vol. 31, No. 1, Winter 2000, pp. 23–39.

List, John A., W. Warren McHone, and Daniel L. Millimet, "Effects of Air Quality Regulation on the Destination Choice of Relocating Plants," *Oxford Economic Papers*, Vol. 55, 2003, pp. 657–678.

List, John A., Daniel L. Millimet, Per G. Fredriksson, and W. Warren McHone, "Effects of Environmental Regulations on Manufacturing Plant Births: Evidence from a Propensity Score Matching Estimator," *Review of Economics and Statistics*, Vol. 85, No. 4, November 2003, pp. 944–952.

List, John A., Daniel L. Millimet, and Warren McHone, "The Unintended Disincentive in the Clean Air Act," *B. E. Journal of Economic Analysis and Policy*, Vol. 3, No. 2, February 2004, pp. 1–28.

Luechinger, Simon, "Valuing Air Quality Using the Life Satisfaction Approach," *Economic Journal*, Vol. 119, No. 536, March 2009, pp. 482–515.

———, "Life Satisfaction and Transboundary Air Pollution," *Economics Letters*, Vol. 107, No. 1, April 2010, pp. 4–6.

Malecki, Edward J., and Susan L. Bradbury, "R&D Facilities and Professional Labour: Labour Force Dynamics in High Technology," *Regional Studies*, Vol. 26, No. 2, 1992, pp. 123–136.

Menzies, Dick, Joe Pasztor, Fatima Nunes, Jeff Leduc, and Chun-Ho Chan, "Effect of a New Ventilation System on Health and Well- Being of Office Workers," *Archives of Environmental Health*, Vol. 52, No. 5, 1997, pp. 360–367.

Milton, Donald K., P. Mark Glencross, and Michael D. Walters, "Risk of Sick Leave Associated with Outdoor Air Supply Rate, Humidification, and Occupant Complaints," *Indoor Air*, Vol. 10, No. 4, 2000, pp. 212–221.

Mohai, Paul, Byoung-Suk Kweon, Sangyun Lee, and Kerry Ard, "Air Pollution Around Schools Is Linked to Poorer Student Health and Academic Performance," *Health Affairs*, Vol. 30, No. 5, May 2011, pp. 852–862.

Moonie, Sheniz, David A. Sterling, Larry W. Figgs, and Mario Castro, "The Relationship Between School Absence, Academic Performance, and Asthma Status," *Journal of School Health*, Vol. 78, No. 3, March 2008, pp. 140–148.

Morgan, O. Ashton, and Simon Condliffe, "Spatial Heterogeneity in Environmental Regulation Enforcement and the Firm Location Decision Among U.S. Counties," *Review of Regional Studies*, Vol. 39. No. 3, 2009, pp. 239–252.

Morgenstern, Richard D., William A. Pizer, and Jhih-Shyang Shih, "Jobs Versus the Environment: An Industry-Level Perspective," *Journal of Environmental Economics and Management*, Vol. 43, No. 3, May 2002, pp. 412–436.

National Center for Environmental Assessment, Research Triangle Park Office, Office of Research and Development, U.S. Environmental Protection Agency, *Air Quality Criteria for Ozone and Related Photochemical Oxidants: Volume I of III*, Research Triangle Park, N.C., EPA 600/R-05/004aF, February 2006. As of November 5, 2013:
http://purl.access.gpo.gov/GPO/LPS86552

Neidell, Matthew, "Public Information and Avoidance Behavior: Do People Respond to Smog Alerts?" working paper, October 2006.

Neild, Ruth Curran, and Robert Balfanz, *Unfulfilled Promise: The Dimensions and Characteristics of Philadelphia's Dropout Crisis, 2000–2005*, Baltimore, Md.: Center for Social Organization of Schools, Johns Hopkins University, October 2006. As of November 13, 2013:
http://www.csos.jhu.edu/new/Neild_Balfanz_06.pdf

Nelson, Randy A., Tom Tietenberg, and Michael R. Donihue, "Differential Environmental Regulation: Effects on Electric Utility Capital Turnover and Emissions," *Review of Economics and Statistics*, Vol. 75, No. 2, May 1993, pp. 368–373.

Nettleman, M. D., T. White, S. Lavoie, and C. Chafin, "School Absenteeism, Parental Work Loss, and Acceptance of Childhood Influenza Vaccination," *American Journal of the Medical Sciences*, Vol. 321, No. 3, April 2001, pp. 178–180.

Neuzil, Kathleen M., Cynthia Hohlbein, and Yuwei Zhu, "Illness Among Schoolchildren During Influenza Season: Effect on School Absenteeism, Parental Absenteeism from Work, and Secondary Illness in Families," *Archives of Pediatric and Adolescent Medicine*, Vol. 156, No. 10, 2002, pp. 986–991.

Nichols, Joe D., "Prediction Indicators for Students Failing the State of Indiana High School Graduation Exam," *Preventing School Failure*, Vol. 47, No. 3, 2003, pp. 112–120.

Office of Management and Budget, *Revised Delineations of Metropolitan Statistical Areas, Micropolitan Statistical Areas, and Combined Statistical Areas, and Guidance on Uses of the Delineations of These Areas*, Washington, D.C., Bulletin 13-01, February 28, 2013. As of November 5, 2013: http://www.whitehouse.gov/sites/default/files/omb/bulletins/2013/b-13-01.pdf

Ostro, Bart D., "Air Pollution and Morbidity Revisited: A Specification Test," *Journal of Environmental Economics and Management*, Vol. 14, No. 1, March 1987, pp. 87–98.

Ostro, Bart D., and Susy Rothschild, "Air Pollution and Acute Respiratory Morbidity: An Observational Study of Multiple Pollutants," *Environmental Research*, Vol. 50, No. 2, December 1989, pp. 238–247.

Ozone Secretariat, United Nations Environment Programme, Montreal Protocol on Substances That Deplete the Ozone Layer, September 15, 1988. As of November 8, 2013: http://ozone.unep.org/new_site/en/Treaties/treaties_decisions-hb.php?nav_id=2094

Palmer, Karen, Wallace E. Oates, and Paul R. Portney, "Tightening Environmental Standards: The Benefit-Cost or No-Cost Paradigm?" *Journal of Economic Perspectives*, Vol. 9, No. 4, Autumn 1995, pp. 119–132.

PDE—*See* Pennsylvania Department of Education.

Pennsylvania Department of Education, *Child Accounting Data Files and Reports: Average Daily Attendance, 2008–2009*, c. 2009. As of August 2, 2013: http://www.education.state.pa.us/portal/server.pt/community/reports_and_data_files/14671

Peters, A., D. W. Dockery, J. Heinrich, and H. E. Wichmann, "Short-Term Effects of Particulate Air Pollution on Respiratory Morbidity in Asthmatic Children," *European Respiratory Journal*, Vol. 10, 1997, pp. 872–879.

"Pittsburgh," *Encyclopedia Britannica Online*, undated. As of August 1, 2013: http://www.britannica.com/EBchecked/topic/462222/Pittsburgh

Popp, David, "International Innovation and Diffusion of Air Pollution Control Technologies: The Effects of NOX and SO2 Regulation in the US, Japan, and Germany," *Journal of Environmental Economics and Management*, Vol. 51, No. 1, January 2006, pp. 46–71.

Porell, Frank W., "Intermetropolitan Migration and Quality of Life," *Journal of Regional Science*, Vol. 22, No. 2, May 1982, pp. 137–158.

Porter, Michael E., and Claas van der Linde, "Toward a New Conception of the Environment-Competitiveness Relationship," *Journal of Economic Perspectives*, Vol. 9, No. 4, 1995, pp. 97–118.

Public Law 88-206, Clean Air Act, December 17, 1963. As of November 5, 2013: http://www.gpo.gov/fdsys/pkg/STATUTE-77/pdf/STATUTE-77-Pg392.pdf

Public Law 101-549, Clean Air Act Amendments, November 15, 1990.

Ransom, Michael R., and C. Arden Pope III, "Elementary School Absences and PM10 Pollution in Utah Valley," *Environmental Research*, Vol. 58, No. 1–2, June–August 1992, pp. 204–219.

Rizzo, Michael, Air Quality Data Analysis Group, Office of Air Quality Planning and Standards, U.S. Environmental Protection Agency, "A Comparison Between Different Rollback Methodologies Applied to Ambient Ozone Concentrations," memorandum to the Ozone National Ambient Air Quality Standards Review Docket EPA-HQ-OAR-0172-0005, November 7, 2005. As of November 5, 2013: http://epa.gov/ttn/naaqs/standards/ozone/data/rizzo-memo-11-05.pdf

———, "A Distributional Comparison Between Different Rollback Methodologies Applied to Ambient Ozone Concentrations," memo to the Ozone NAAQS Review Docket, EPA-HQ-OAR-0172-0027, August 23, 2006. As of November 13, 2013:
http://www.epa.gov/ttn/naaqs/standards/ozone/data/20060823_rizzo_rollback_evaluation.pdf

Roby, Douglas E., "Research on School Attendance and Student Achievement: A Study of Ohio Schools," *Educational Research Quarterly*, Vol. 28, No. 1, September 2004, pp. 3–16.

Romieu, Isabelle, Marlene Cortes Lugo, Silvia Ruiz Velasco, Sergio Sanchez, Fermando Meneses, and Mauricio Hemandez, "Air Pollution and School Absenteeism Among Children in Mexico City," *American Journal of Epidemiology*, Vol. 136, No. 12, 1992, pp. 1524–1531.

Rumberger, Russell W., and Scott L. Thomas, "The Distribution of Dropout and Turnover Rates Among Urban and Suburban High Schools," *Sociology of Education*, Vol. 73, No. 1, January 2000, pp. 39–67.

Salvesen, David, and Henry Renski, *The Importance of Quality of Life in the Location Decisions of New Economy Firms*, Chapel Hill, N.C.: Center for Urban and Regional Studies, January 2003. As of November 5, 2013:
https://curs.unc.edu/files/2013/04/neweconomyreport.pdf

Silverstein, M. D., J. E. Mair, S. K. Katusic, P. C. Wollan, E. J. O'Connell, and J. W. Yunginger, "School Attendance and School Performance: A Population-Based Study of Children with Asthma," *Journal of Pediatrics*, Vol. 139, No. 2, August 2001, pp. 278–283.

Smith, V. Kerry, and Ju-Chin Huang, "Can Markets Value Air Quality? A Meta-Analysis of Hedonic Property Value Models," *Journal of Political Economy*, Vol. 103, No. 1, February 1995, pp. 209–227.

U.S. Census Bureau, *The 2012 Statistical Abstract: The National Data Book*, 2012a. As of August 2, 2013:
http://www.census.gov/compendia/statab/

———, "County Business Patterns," last revised October 28, 2013; referenced October 1, 2012b. As of November 5, 2013:
http://www.census.gov/econ/cbp/

———, "American FactFinder," undated; referenced November 2012c. As of November 5, 2013:
http://factfinder2.census.gov/

———, "North American Industry Classification System: Concordances," last revised September 13, 2013; referenced August 2, 2013. As of November 5, 2013:
http://www.census.gov/eos/www/naics/concordances/concordances.html

U.S. Code, Title 42, The Public Health and Welfare, Chapter 85, Air Pollution Prevention and Control, Section 7401, Congressional Findings and Declaration of Purpose. As of November 6, 2013:
http://www.gpo.gov/fdsys/pkg/USCODE-2010-title42/html/USCODE-2010-title42-chap85.htm

U.S. Department of the Interior and U.S. Geological Survey, "Pennsylvania: Counties," *The National Atlas of the United States of America*, undated. As of November 5, 2013:
http://www.nationalatlas.gov/printable/images/pdf/counties3/pagecnty_pa3.pdf

U.S. Environmental Protection Agency, Office of Air and Radiation and Office of Policy, *The Benefits and Costs of the Clean Air Act, 1990 to 2010: EPA Report to Congress*, Washington, D.C., EPA-410-R-99-001, November 1999. As of November 5, 2013:
http://purl.access.gpo.gov/GPO/LPS18545

———, "National Ambient Air Quality Standards for Ozone," *Federal Register*, Vol. 73, No. 60, March 27, 2008, pp. 16436–16514. As of November 13, 2013:
http://www.gpo.gov/fdsys/pkg/FR-2008-03-27/pdf/E8-5645.pdf

———, *Integrated Science Assessment for Particulate Matter (Final Report)*, Washington, D.C., EPA/600/R-08/139F, December 2009. As of November 5, 2013:
http://cfpub.epa.gov/ncea/cfm/recordisplay.cfm?deid=216546

———, *Integrated Science Assessment for Carbon Monoxide (Final Report)*, Washington, D.C., EPA/600/R-09/019F, January 2010. As of November 5, 2013:
http://cfpub.epa.gov/ncea/cfm/recordisplay.cfm?deid=218686

———, *The Benefits and Costs of the Clean Air Act from 1990 to 2020*, March 2011a.

———, *Regulatory Impact Analysis for the Final Mercury and Air Toxics Standards*, Washington, D.C., EPA-452/R-11-011, December 2011b. As of November 5, 2013:
http://purl.fdlp.gov/GPO/gpo38996

———, "National Ambient Air Quality Standards," last updated December 14, 2012. As of September 18, 2013:
http://www.epa.gov/air/criteria.html

———, *Integrated Science Assessment for Ozone and Related Photochemical Oxidants (Final Report)*, Washington, D.C., EPA/600/R-10/076F, February 2013a. As of August 2, 2013:
http://cfpub.epa.gov/ncea/isa/recordisplay.cfm?deid=247492

———, *Integrated Science Assessment for Lead (Final Report)*, Washington, D.C., June 2013b. As of August 2, 2013:
http://cfpub.epa.gov/ncea/isa/recordisplay.cfm?deid=255721

———, "2005 National-Scale Air Toxics Assessment," last updated May 21, 2012; referenced July 2013c. As of November 5, 2013:
http://www.epa.gov/nata2005/

———, *The Green Book Nonattainment Areas for Criteria Pollutants*, July 31, 2013d. As of November 6, 2013:
http://www.epa.gov/airquality/greenbook/

———, "About Air Toxics," last updated August 8, 2013e. As of November 13, 2013:
http://www.epa.gov/ttn/atw/allabout.html

———, "Design Values in Areas Previously Designated Nonattainment for the 2008 8-Hour Ozone NAAQS," 2012 design value report for ozone, Table 1a, last updated July 1, 2013; referenced November 12, 2013f. As of November 12, 2013:
http://www.epa.gov/airtrends/values.html

———, "Design Values in Areas Previously Designated Nonattainment for the 1997 PM2.5 Annual NAAQS," 2012 design value report for particulate matter less than 2.5 microns in diameter, Table 1a, last updated August 9, 2013; referenced November 12, 2013g. As of November 12, 2013:
http://www.epa.gov/airtrends/values.html

———, "Technology Transfer Network (TTN) Air Quality System (AQS)," last updated August 27, 2013h. As of November 13, 2013:
http://www.epa.gov/ttn/airs/airsaqs/

———, "Regulatory Actions," last updated September 24, 2013i. As of October 31, 2013:
http://www.epa.gov/glo/actions.html

Walker, W. Reed, *The Transitional Costs of Sectoral Reallocation: Evidence from the Clean Air Act and the Workforce*, working paper, 2012.

Wargocki, Pawel, David P. Wyon, Jan Sundell, Geo Clausen, and P. Ole Fanger, "The Effects of Outdoor Air Supply Rate in an Office on Perceived Air Quality, Sick Building Syndrome (SBS) Symptoms and Productivity," *Indoor Air*, Vol. 10, 2000, pp. 222–236.

Welsch, Heinz, "Environment and Happiness: Valuation of Air Pollution Using Life Satisfaction Data," *Ecological Economics*, Vol. 58, No. 4, July 1, 2006, pp. 801–813.

Wyon, D. P., "The Effects of Indoor Air Quality on Performance and Productivity," *Indoor Air*, Vol. 14, Suppl. 7, 2004, pp. 92–101.

Zweig, Jacqueline S., John C. Ham, and Edward L. Avol, *Air Pollution and Academic Performance: Evidence from California Schools*, working paper, December 2009. As of December 2012: http://econweb.umd.edu/~ham/test%20scores%20submit.pdf